PRIDE OF PLACE

A CONTEMPORARY ANTHOLOGY OF TEXAS NATURE WRITING

EDITED BY DAVID TAYLOR

D1565864

UNIVERSITY OF NORTH TEXAS PRESS
DENTON, TEXAS

10 9 8 7 6 5 4 3 2 1

Permissions:
University of North Texas Press
P.O. Box 311336
Denton, TX 76203-1336

The paper used in this book meets the minimum requirements of the American National Standard for Permanence of Paper for Printed Library Materials, z39.48.1984. Binding materials have been chosen for durability.

Library of Congress Cataloging-in-Publication Data

Pride of place : a contemporary anthology of Texas nature writing / edited by David Taylor.
p. cm.
Includes index.
ISBN-13: 978-1-57441-207-9 (cloth : alk. paper)
ISBN-10: 1-57441-207-8 (cloth : alk. paper)
ISBN-13: 978-1-57441-208-6 (pbk. : alk. paper)
ISBN-10: 1-57441-208-6 (pbk. : alk. paper)
1. Natural history--Texas. I. Taylor, David, 1962-
QH105.T4P76 2006
508.764--dc22
                              2005028382
Cover Image "Big Bend" is by Wyman Meinzer.

DEDICATION

*To my parents for their unconditional love and support.
They are Texans in the very biggest and best sense.*

All things that are alive

are brothers in the soil and in the sky

and I believe it with my blood

if not my eyes.

—Townes Van Zandt,
"High, Low, and In Between"

CONTENTS

Acknowledgments

Some of the essays have appeared previously. They are as follows:

"Still Water"
From *Adventures with a Texas Naturalist* by Roy Bedichek, Copyright © 1947, 1961, renewed 1989. By permission of the University of Texas Press.

"Kindred Spirits"
From *From a Limestone Ledge: Some Essays and Other Ruminations about Country Life in Texas*, published by Southern Methodist University Press, and originally in hardcover by Alfred A. Knopf. Copyright © 1980 by John Graves. Reprinted by permission of the author.

"That One-Eyed Hereford Muley"
From *The Wild and the Domestic: Animal Representation, Ecocriticism, and Western American Literature* by Barney Nelson. Copyright © 2000 by University of Nevada Press. Reprinted with the permission of the University of Nevada Press.

"Tortas Locas"
From *The Underground Heart: A Return to a Hidden Landscape*, by Ray Gonzales. Copyright © 2002 by Ray Gonzales. Reprinted by permission of the University of Arizona Press.

"Home Address"
From *Never in a Hurry: Essays on People and Places*, by Naomi Shihab Nye. Copyright © 1996 by Naomi Shihab Nye. Reprinted by permission of the University of South Carolina Press.

"Faith's Place" by Gerald Thurmond
From *Crossroads: A Southern Culture Annual*, ed. by Ted Olson. Copyright © 2005 by Mercer University Press. Reprinted by permission of Mercer University Press.

All such collections are the product of the labor and caring of many people. First and foremost, I would like to thank Karen DeVinney, Managing Editor of UNT Press, whose patience and kindness toward this project and me have made its publication possible.

The authors have endured countless emails, letters, requests, and suggestions and stayed in good spirits. A deep thanks goes to them.

I also want to thank my family: my daughter Kory, my parents Dene and Eugene Taylor, my brother Don and sister Debra and their families, Connie, Jessica, as well as the whole Peden clan. My love to you all.

The Center for Environmental Philosophy has been extremely generous to me over the last three years. Eugene Hargrove and Jan Dickson have been not only wonderful colleagues, but great friends. Thanks to Mary Autry for typing several of the essays.

Last, my return to Denton has given me the chance to renew many old friendships and further close ones. None has been so dear to me over the years than that of my friend Scott Schram. His wisdom and caring matter immeasurably to me.

INTRODUCTION

I've long thought about this project—an anthology of Texas nature writing. As a child I grew up below the Lake Lewisville dam and spent lots of hours wandering around in the flood plains of the Elm Fork. Lewisville was then a rural town—the downtown feed mill still a vital part of the community and town economics, and the same red, white, and blue bunting used for all town holidays from the Fourth of July rodeo to the homecoming parade.

Family vacations included trips to Sam Rayburn Lake, Goose Island, the Big Thicket, Palo Duro Canyon, and once to El Paso. As a child I thought the distance between these destinations as far as to another planet, since only a ranch here and there or fields of cotton, corn, or sorghum dotted the forested and desert spaces between towns. As anyone who has lived in Texas for any time will tell you, most of it's changed. Fewer spaces between towns, and the dots have become convenience stores, which soon add a fast food place and then mature into strip malls. Sure, if you drive out west far enough or spend enough time looking for back roads, you'll get a sense of what it was, but what was the rule is now the exception.

What's stirred me to bring this writing together isn't nostalgia or anti-development sentiments, though I hold both of those. Instead, it is that wonder I'd slip into as a child about the vast spaces of Texas landscapes as we traveled. The family vehicle was a 1967 Chevrolet pickup; after 100 miles or so, Mom and Dad would tire of listening to the three kids and banish us to the bed of the truck. My use of the word "bed" is literal, as dad had placed a mattress in the back with a camper top shielding us from the elements, excepting heat of course. Much of the time we vied for a breeze, placing our faces near the two slatted windows; I being the youngest waited on the largesse of my two older siblings to offer access to a window—that and if I got sick or whined too much they knew there'd be hell to pay when Dad stopped the truck. But in those times when we'd pass a few hundred miles at a time without too much discomfort, I could slip into a reverie about what was passing by—pines, swamps, bays, lakes, rivers, coast, oaks, bluebonnets, longhorns, mesquite, prairie, hills, prickly pear, mule ear, cholla, an ochre sunset on the Davis Mountains. Watching them was hypnotic, but these trances were interrupted by a coyote sighting, the searing color of wild-flower fields, antelope out west, or a whooping crane down by the coast. I knew there was something important in allowing myself to silently take all these things in, and as I have grown older, I see myself finding times to be that boy taking in not just scenery but place. It is that reverie that brought me to love these places, to worry for them, and to write and work for them as well.

We must take up a few considerations about an anthology that uses state borders as its literary and geographical boundary. Let me begin with a few of these:

I've never been much on the idea of state borders—this airy notion of longitude or latitude is one state, and an inch or so the other way is another. The greatest value I've seen of this kind of geography is watching previously reserved folks at Four Corners allow loved ones to take public pictures of them in awkward and compromising positions, just to say they'd been in four states at once.

I guess I like the idea of river borders better than drawn ones. I can sense one riverbank from another. This human ideal of boundaries conforms better to the phenomenon of bank-river-bank. This is my side; that is your side. The problem with river borders is that depending upon the precipitation, someone's side is increasing or decreasing.

Channels can move a border this way or that, depending upon a flood or mood of a river, and the fact that natural features can still cause political consternation brings me a certain joy. The Red River boundary was disputed for years. In 1999, in a hearing before the Subcommittee on Commercial and Administrative Law, a Texas House Representative wrote,

> The boundary is an artificial line in that it must be located
> by a survey, and that may move due to changes in the river,

and if it is marked, the markers will be removed by the river over time and may not be on line if the river changes. The boundary is thus inappropriate for a jurisdictional line between the States.[1]

The compromise was to make the southern vegetation line as the official border. Let's see what global warming will do to that one.

All this is to say that jurisdictional borders are good for laws, taxes, and property lines, maybe even college football games, but they don't do much for saying anything really important about a place. Thus, with the task of putting together an anthology of nature writing from our state, calling it "Texas" nature writing and using its borders is at best arbitrary and at worst, just plain silly.[2]

Using bioregions (an area of similar weather, land, water, plants, and critters) is more accurate to the spirit of a nature anthology: that the stories be drawn from similar landscape. However, this would leave Texans needing to buy at least eleven anthologies instead of one. Our "borders" are home to the Piney Woods, Oak Woods and Prairies, Blackland Prairies, Gulf Coast Prairies and Marshes, Coastal Sand Plains, South Texas Brush Country, Edwards Plateau, Llano Uplift, Rolling Plains, High Plains, and Trans Pecos bioregions.[3] Too, if we adhere to the idea that landscape shapes people as much as people shape landscape, then we're also left pondering the distance between a West Texas cowboy and bayou, alligator folk in Southeast Texas, much less what they have to say to each other about their nature writing. So what might we say holds these works together? Why an anthology of writing chosen by human boundaries?

"Don't Mess with Texas"—Pride, Identity, and Being Native

There is very little that binds us here in Texas. We may talk about music, cowboys, big cars, big hair, boots, open landscapes, and forests, but each of these reflects only a part of Texas, very little about its glue. About the closest thing one can say that makes us Texan is our pride *in being* Texans. Many have conjectured as to its mysterious roots: the Alamo, our years as a Republic, the rugged landscape, the cattle boom, the Comanche and desperado past, the oil boom, our sense of always being something a little more than just a state. Most likely this intense pride is a combination of the above and now finds itself passed on through the remaining "native" Texans as a badge of distinction or a marketing gimmick. Think back to the "New York City?" picante/salsa commercials of the '90s. Consider most of pickup truck ads. None needs to distinguish itself as set in Texas; that is a given, as dust roils from the spinning back wheels, as a rancher throws a bale of hay from the bed, and tosses the gear in the back at the end of the day. That Texas functions in the minds of Texans, if not most Americans, as a defined place without noting it says something about its unique cultural place in our mythologies. Texas bravado belies our own sense that what we take pride in isn't one particular landscape but the whole. What we take pride in **is** its size. Stephen Harrigan in "What Texas Means to Me" writes:

> Texas is a zone in which the stunning vistas more or less peter out, leaving us with only one great geographical distinction: size. The prudent and prideful Texan takes in the whole package while retaining an affection for the few component parts with the necessary spit and polish to be thought of as scenery. He develops an eye for breadth…[4]

The political boundaries and borders that define Texas are so vast and so diverse that an immense pride is a way to find common ground. This conceit evokes what most of us already know: bravado equals pride, communal pride equals community, and communities make choices about what they are and how they look.

The best environmental example of this choice has been Texas Department of Transportation's (TxDOT's) "Don't Mess with Texas" anti-litter campaign. The campaign was launched in 1986 after research had shown that most people littering were between the ages of 18 and 34. The ads combined an in-your-face attitude, a nice rhyme, and a broad accusation. It was an overnight success, as Stevie Ray Vaughan droned out the lyrics with a dare. Others include notable musicians (Willie Nelson and the Fabulous Thunderbirds), famous athletes (Randy White and George Foreman), and public figures. In a short five years, littering had been reduced by 72%. Why litter declined is less ostensibly about Texans embracing an environmental perspective, than it is the "Don't Mess with Texas" honing in on Texas pride and using it as a means. However, it also touches upon an unspoken aspect of Texas pride; if we truly take such pride in our state, then shouldn't we take better care of it? TxDot sums it:

> What others have called braggadocio we Texans call pride…
> after all, "It ain't braggin' if it's true." We're crazy about our
> home state and we want the world to know it.[5]

The brilliance of the campaign rests on understanding the role of narrative in a culture or community. Communities (families, neighborhoods, towns, states, and even nations) define themselves by story, whether with braggadocio or some other tone. As one taps into that cultural story and ties a positive community concern (here, anti-littering) to it, the more the story affirms community in its effectiveness. In other words, every time someone rattles off "Don't Mess with Texas," it not only reaffirms Texas mythology, it adds to it the thread of putting trash where it belongs.

Thus, much of what holds these essays together comes from this story of Texas pride: that we and the landscape are important and worthy of pride, if not bravado. We too often apply the name "Native Texan" to those who were born and grew up here, but being "Native" is more about learning to listen, to laugh, and to use such stories, than where we first saw light. Learning to speak within the stories of a community is the way one becomes a part of that community. Adding one's unique perspective and concerns broadens the story and strengthens the community too. My hope is this anthology will serve just this purpose for the reader: to reaffirm Texas' cultural stories of nature, to broaden their scope with lots of different perspectives and landscapes, and to draw from them a value of respect and caring we already, but indirectly, express.

Translating Value into Ethics—How Stories Can Become Choice

I grew up a Fundamental Independent Baptist, which mostly meant we thought that Southern Baptists were too liberal. You needn't guess where that put Episcopalians and Catholics. Our weekly sermons drew from the Old Testament, stories of God's direct actions and tales of human frailty and woe. I still think Job the everyman. The literary term we call these sermons is a "jeremiad": a story decrying the present woeful state of affairs, looking back to when things were right, and calling for listeners/readers to commit themselves to change. Most of us who have attended a church, synagogue, mosque, and sometimes even Unitarian gatherings, know this story. American nature writers and environmentalists have used it for over two hundred years, as forests were felled, rivers polluted, air quality lost, damaging pesticides introduced, and on and on. If actions keep going this way, they say, we are headed for ruin. This isn't to say that these stories aren't factual. How would life be in the US without Rachel Carson's *Silent Spring*? What I'm suggesting is that one of the reasons these stories have worked is that they tapped into a cultural storyline most of us already knew through our religious backgrounds. We knew the story as we were reading it.

However, it's a difficult thing to say that they also embedded an environmental ethic into American minds. Traditional philosophy examines ethics as the systematic study of making a right choice or a wrong one. These studies have branched into lots of theoretical possibilities (virtue, duty, etc.) and have also been applied to practical concerns: medical, social, and environmental. The latter has become an academic field of study within the last twenty-five years. Most of this applied philosophy is expressed within the rhetoric and style of academic scholarship: expository, documented, and formal. Many of these ethical studies have had influence over policy decisions, the shape of research, and administrative oversight, but few have been directly involved in a community's ethical choice concerning the environment. Most often, a broader community's choices are influenced by narrative: *Walden, Sand County Almanac, Silent Spring,* and *Monkey Wrench Gang,* for example. These are often deeply informed by ethical considerations, but it is the ability to bind these considerations to a lived mythology that gives them personal and communal resonance. As Pete Gunter and Max Oelschlaeger say in *Texas Land Ethics*:

> a land ethic involves us in our natural world and orients us toward fruitful ways of living in it without wrecking it. Beyond this, philosophy and ethic cannot go. They orient us in general, fruitful ways. Experience, common sense, and the natural and social sciences must fill in the details. No philosophy can deduce the particulars of our experience.[6]

Narrative and story, however, can bring it closer to our home.

Look back at the "Don't Mess with Texas" campaign. While its long-term environmental efficacy is more cosmetic than structural, its effectiveness cannot be denied. Thus, in Texas, we've too long let the story of private property rights override our competing narrative, state pride—not just in our piece of Texas but all of it, in its shared concept. I am not suggesting we repeal private property rights. What I'm saying is the ethic of shared responsibility for our state expressed in "Don't Mess with Texas" is as much what we are responding to as the bravado. Thus, when it comes to some difficult environmental choices about water rights, land use, sprawl, etc., we need our mythologies and stories to help us incorporate all the facts, philosophies, policies, and sentiments that make up a quality decision. Stories can and do ground these issues by spanning the individual, scientific, and monetary concerns by linking them with a story that we already know and already live. This collection carries with it, then, the story of pride, attention, the detail of a place, the expanse of a myth, and, inevitably for the reader, choice. How that choice is enacted is both personal and communal.

A Tradition of Texas Nature Writing—Bedichek and Graves

The area that now comprises Texas was relatively well traversed by natives and non-natives in the years before and after its independence and statehood, and we have a healthy log of journals and notes from early settlers and explorers. Samuel Wood Geiser's *Naturalists of the Frontier* (1948) gives a good overview of the major nineteenth-century naturalists to have completed work in Texas. More recently, Del Weniger's *The Explorer's Texas: The Lands and Waters* does an admirable job of dividing the exploration narratives among specific landforms and rivers and quoting liberally from them to give us a sense of pre-settlement Texas. The style and purpose of these early narratives vary between scientific description, promotional hyperbole, and evangelical wilderness musings. There really isn't much in the way of a tradition in them as one might see in early descriptions of, say, Virginia or Massachusetts. In those locations, well-schooled gentleman naturalists were from nearby centers of education and turned their focus to much smaller areas.[7]

In truth, there was little in the way of a tradition in Texas nature writing until Roy Bedichek. Born in the late nineteenth century, Bedichek's style is drawn from his life of education. His early training was from his father's school; after completing his BS and MA from University of Texas, he held a series of writing and administrative jobs until landing a position with the University Interscholastic League (UIL). Bedichek worked over 30 years for UIL and resigned as director in 1948.

His essays reflect a broad knowledge of the classical literature and thought combined with a folksy style and solid natural history observation. His essays do not come from the style of the solitary gentleman naturalist so much as from a classically trained and good-hearted neighbor. He introduces Thomas Mann's and Plato's thoughts to his essays (as in "Cedar Cutter") with no more professorial tone than most of us talk about the weather or how our lawns are doing. This tone is reflected in the public persona of Bedichek as well: his close friendships with Frank Dobie and Walter Prescott Webb, philosopher's rock at Barton Springs, and his voluminous correspondence.

Also separating Bedichek's writing from earlier narratives is his craftsmanship of the essay form. *Adventures with a Texas Naturalist* (1947) came from a yearlong leave of absence allowing him to focus solely on his writing. The essays do not rely on journey or observation alone; instead, they develop a broader theme (death, for example, in "Cedar Cutter") in which relevant details of observation, journey, and classical thought are brought into a carefully wrought essay. What Bedichek did was to formalize nature writing in Texas by being the first to make it a recognizable literary genre.

The other legacy Bedichek has given us is attention to the commonplace. Whether the armadillo beneath his house or a mockingbird's call, Bedichek showed readers how to pay close attention to the things and places we take for granted. Valuing the commonplace is important in Texas nature writing, as much of our landscape requires just that to value it—attention. It is far easier to stir a reader's fancy about Big Bend, the Guadalupe Mountains, the Big Thicket, or Padre Island than it is to get them to slow down and see the beauty of the areas around Houston, Dallas-Fort Worth, or Amarillo. Bedichek could find equal relevance and resonance in the wildest of places and his own backyard: it is the attention that matters to him, the caring and pride one has with a place. He concludes the Introduction to *Adventures with a Texas Naturalist*:

> To take a single instance out of those hundreds ready at hand: what a large percentage of urbanized populations miss beginning the day under the spell of the silent, pervasive, leisurely preparations of the heavens to receive the sun![8]

The sentence suggests an ambivalence that continues through much of Texas nature writing: a good deal of optimism tempered by a healthy realism about the ways most of us get by on a daily basis.

Over the last forty years, no one in Texas letters has better captured this complexity of our relationship with our place better than John Graves. From his seminal *Goodbye to a River* (1960) to his collections of essays *Hardscrabble* (1974) and *From a Limestone Ledge* (1980) to the numerous stories, introductions, and forewords, John Graves has given readers a sober view of both our love for and abuse of the natural place of Texas. As Pete Gunter told me, what Graves has done is to articulate the tragedy of our relationship to place.

Tragedy in its literary tradition is the story of a hero, a person of character who tries his darnedest to do good, but from some native-born flaw, most often *hubris* (excess pride), his actions spell his, and often others', inevitable end. What Graves understands is that many of us who love this place—Texans and Texas—end up doing harm, sometimes even from the very pride that could also move us to act more wisely toward the nonhuman. It is a somber story and one that can easily turn to pessimism. In an essay in *Texas Parks & Wildlife*, Graves writes, "in view of what we know about the many forces that continue to hack and tear at the fabric of nature, optimism about long-term prospects is bound to be a bit queasy."[9]

But tragedy in its classical form also offers the hope of *catharsis*, or healing, for the audience. They can see the flaw of the hero in their own lives, embrace the suffering that it has caused the hero and themselves, and purge the anger, fear, and loss. Graves continues:

> none of that [environmental regulations] will mean very much unless a majority of the persons who seek their pleasure outdoors come to understand the scheme of nature to care about it not ignorantly but with knowledge, and in consequence to act decently and responsibly toward it, demanding others do the same.[10]

This tone is the central impression of Graves' nature writing, a clear sense of the strengths of what we are and what we have here in Texas and just as clear a sense of how our ignorance and short-sighted pride are leading to its loss. What the reader sees then in Graves is as deep a love for humanity as for the natural world, a respect for those who have made the tough journey of learning how to live here as sustainably and knowledgeably as possible.

The Tradition Expanded

Readers of this anthology will note that I have not included a number of superb Texas nature writers. Their exclusion is no reflection on their merit or significance in Texas letters. I encourage readers to pick up a copy of *Falling from Grace: A Literary Response to the Demise of Paradise* (Wings Press 2004) for further study.

Readers will also notice many of the following 14 selections discuss the manmade world as readily as they discuss the nonhuman. Homes, restaurants, families, domestic animals, automobiles, towns, and cities are detailed along with the flora, fauna, waterforms, and landforms of Texas. I expect that this will cause some readers consternation, an anthology of nature writing with so much humanity in it. To those, I admit my guilt but offer no apology.

As I wrote earlier, my intent with *Pride of Place* is to bring to light Texas' cultural stories of place and nature, to broaden their scope with lots of different perspectives and landscapes, and to suggest in them a value of respect and caring we Texans already, but indirectly, express. This respect and caring may have begun by a solitary spiritual experience, a hunting or fishing trip, or in watching the loss of another prairie, wood, or stream; it may have started in seeing another small town ravaged by sprawl or a neighborhood lost to some other development. Some of the essays discuss wilderness and the threats it faces; others examine the snake in the backyard, or the river with dumpsites along it. In all of the essays, though, there is a consistency of perspective. Repeated themes include: attention, careful thoughts about the human community and its effects on the nonhuman, an awe and reverence of the nonhuman, and a certain quirkiness arising from our ambivalence about and love for place. As pride in our state has given us a source of identity, it also has the potential to reshape our relationship to nature. I invite readers to engage in this shared and emerging story.

---

1. Subcommittee on Commercial and Administrative Law, *Consent of the Congress to the Red River Compact*, 116th Cong., 1st sess., 1999, 17.

2. Two other Texas collections use state borders as the dividing line similar to this anthology: Howard Peacock, ed., *The Nature of Texas: A Feast of Native Beauty* (College Station: Texas A&M University Press, 1990) and Rick Bass and Paul Christensen, eds. *Falling from Grace in Texas: A Literary Response to the Demise of Paradise* (San Antonio: Wings Press, 2004).

3. The best anthology dedicated to a particular place is Barney Nelson's *God's Country or Devil's Playground: An Anthology of Nature Writing from the Big Bend of Texas* (Austin: University of Texas Press, 2002).

4. Stephen Harrigan, *A Natural State* (Austin: Texas Monthly Press, 1988), 175.

5. Don't Mess with Texas Campaign, Texas Department of Transportation, www.dontmesswith texas.org

6. Pete A.Y. Gunter and Max Oelschlaeger, *Texas Land Ethics* (Austin: University of Texas Press, 1997), 135.

7. Frederick Law Olmstead's *A Journey through Texas: Or, a Saddle-Trip on the Southwestern Frontier* (Austin: University of Texas Press, 1978) is a notable exception.

8. Roy Bedichek, *Adventures with a Texas Naturalist* (Austin: University of Texas Press, 1989), xxviii.

9. John Graves, "Essay for State of Nature: A 50th Anniversary Celebration," *Texas Parks & Wildlife* 50, no.12 (1992): 75.

10. *Ibid.* 77.

Bluebonnets, David Taylor

CHAPTER 1

ROY BEDICHEK

STILL WATER

Roy Bedichek (1878–1959) was the author of four books: *Adventures with a Texas Naturalist* (1947); *Karankaway Country* (1950); *Educational Competition: The Story of the University Interscholastic League in Texas* (1956); and posthumously *The Sense of Smell* (1960). His *Adventures with a Texas Naturalist* is widely regarded as essential reading for those interested in Texana.

Joy shall be in the bird-lover's heart over one new bird more than over ninety and nine already listed. If the newcomer is found to be nesting in territory well outside his usual breeding range, the event stirs the amateur still more deeply.

I say amateur, since the professional ornithologist through overindulgence tends to become insensible to this pleasure, or, in the manner now fashionable, conceals emotional reactions as bad form or as indicating untrustworthy observation. I sometimes think that we have become dominated by a cult of unemotionalism. We speak of "cold" scientific fact as if temperature had something to do with verity. We assume that strong feeling and sound judgment are incompatible, and regard with suspicion all facts which really excite us.

But surely only the phlegmatic person, professional or amateur, can see the vermilion flycatcher for the first time without a gasp of surprise and pleasure. When, on March 20, I found this vivid bit of color flown here from the Tropics on its own power, it came like an unexpected gift from one of those inspired givers who determine by divination, before you yourself do, just what you want.

Only within the past few years has the vermilion flycatcher been found nesting in central Texas as far north as Austin. Now I hear on good authority that this most striking member of the family of Tyrant flycatchers has been seen lately as far north as Glen Rose. The species is evidently northward bound.

On that March morning the male was showing off, displaying himself advantageously, he hoped, before the eyes of the female of his choice. I found him soaring on wings that "beat the gladsome air," poising, shivering with anticipation, breast feathers all puffed out with pride and confidence.

Although in my eyes he made a creditable exhibition and finished in approved manner, looping gracefully earthward with a final flourish, the female viewed the performance with a more critical eye. He was not immediately accepted. She moved away upon his approach. I spent some time following these lively visitors about and was rewarded by seeing them engage in a flight and pursuit as mad and furious as any of nature's hurdle races with goal set to ravish or devour.

Beautiful in her own quiet way, especially in contrast with her suitor so gorgeously arrayed, I thought of her as modesty itself wooed by an aggressive egotism. Fast and furious was the race amid the tangled vines and branches. Too quick for the eye, first here, then there, dodging with movements indescribably swift, she fled like a gray leaf pursued by a darting tongue of flame. During my observation of them he remained a rejected suitor. Finally they rested quietly within twenty feet of where I was standing.

In a proper light, the female's back appears a dullish gray dusted over with iron rust. Her breast is slightly streaked with brown, the flanks yellowish shading into gray, the throat gray with deeper gray about the cheeks.

It is the male, however, which inspires the naturalist to raptures and to do his best at descriptive writing, seeking until he finds phrases and similitudes with which to set this bird apart from all others as a kind of special creation. He is a brilliant flaming gem, an outburst of gleaming color, and outshines the most brilliant scarlet flowers. To the imaginative Mexicans, he is *brasita de fuego,* a little coal of fire; and his scientific name, *Pyrocephalus,* signifies firehead. Poised high in the crystal-clear air that morning, he seemed to me to be a star of first magnitude which the vanishing darkness had failed to take with it from the daylight sky. All who know tanagers should be advised that after seeing this tropical newcomer, the summer tanager appears faded and even the scarlet tanager seems a bit tame. The gray-tailed cardinal is dull in comparison.

The courting flight of the vermilion flycatcher—tiniest of the tribe except those of the genus Epidonax—this soaring and poising high in the air, would seem to be in deliberate scorn of the whole tribe of hawks, always on the lookout for a small bird to stoop at. But I have never seen a hawk show any interest in him. The flycatchers with the bulldoggish jaws have what is known in the athletic world as the fighting heart, and perhaps this ostentatious flight of the most colorful of the family may be considered as a red flag of defiance hoisted by Tyrannidae to assert its fearlessness, its challenge to all comers to do battle, if they choose, to the last extremity with no holds barred. Even the surly mockingbird shows great respect for flycatchers. The little ball of fire has the flycatcher fight in him. I should think that an observation of the display with which the male endeavors to win the favor of the female would give pause to those literal folk who attempt to reduce the mating of birds to the slot-machine reactions of an automat.

I wish I might report that this pair nested here, but they were only on an exploratory mission. Conditions did not suit them, and after May 2 I saw them no more, although I continued my search for a nest well into June. During their stay on Bear Creek, they occupied a feeding stratum midway between the phoebe and the scissortail. Along the creek and river courses of the Edwards Plateau, the phoebe's favorite feeding perch is a low limb preferably over water; the vermilion feeds from treetops down in the valley, while the scissortail stays on treetops of the more elevated terraces, occasionally taking advantage of a power line as it tops the hill.

The tails of these aerial acrobats are highly mobile, each one, however, with its own distinctive type of mobility. Much has been written of tail shape as an aid in maneuvering, but tail strength and tail mobility also are important. The family is noted for bursts of speed and lightening wheel-abouts rather than for swiftness in sustained flight. The scissortail, for instance, darts like an arrow, but covers a hundred yards at less than twenty miles an hour. Perching, the tail of the vermilion moves fanwise, opening and closing, to maintain balance. The phoebe, on the other hand, raises and lowers its tail as a pipit does, but much more slowly and, so far as I can see, not merely to balance himself but simply because he thinks it becoming to move his tail slowly up and down. He often sits for a long time with no movement of the tail at all and then begins again with great deliberation. It seems more of a mannerism than movement with a purpose. The only other bird I know which, while perching, moves its tail in the same plane and through about the same arc as the phoebe, but with still greater deliberation, is the hermit thrush. The scissortail perching in the wind uses his ten-inch tail as a balance, but in still weather often lets it droop down completely relaxed. It is in flight, turning and twisting in pursuit of prey, or in threatening forays toward intruders coming too near his nest, that his tail takes on the scissoring motion which gives him his name.

There is no doubt that the vermilion flycatcher is extending his range northward, especially in central Texas. Chapman (1912) gives his breeding range as Central America and Mexico, north to southern Texas. Simmons (1925) records only a straggler, a single male, taken March 16, 1914. He predicts, but without giving reasons, that this bird "will probably appear more often and eventually become a rare summer resident." Bent (1942) gives the northern limit of *Pyrocephalus* in Texas as San Antonio. In March 1942 I found a pair on the shore of the new Marshall Ford Lake about six miles above the dam. They spent the whole season there but I did not succeed in finding a nest. The next season I did find a nest in that location and another nesting pair on the Shields Ranch ten miles away. These birds like people: both the nests were near dwellings, one of them within fifty feet of the back door of a ranch house.

The only good thing I ever heard about a South American dictatorship is that the South American form of the vermilion flycatcher is protected by presidential decree.

The reason for the shift in breeding range of a given species is usually obvious. Dry up a marsh and as a matter of course the marsh birds move away. Make a marsh and they naturally flow in. The breaking up of the great, grassy ranches of the Panhandle of Texas has made the upland plover a rather rare bird there except in special locations. On the other hand, we sometimes find in the breeding range of a particular species shifts difficult to explain. I have as yet found no explanation of the European stork's extension of his breeding range during the past fifty years from northern Germany for hundreds of miles into Russia. I have found comments concerning the movement of the Carolina wren into New England, but no explanations.

To find a straggler five hundred or a thousand miles off his usual beat is an exciting incident. On Hearst Creek, ten miles above the Marshall Ford Dam, in 1942, I found the black-throated gray warbler and have bored my more tolerant friends with accounts of this discovery ever since. Such an incident is not worth a headline; but to find year after year a bird changing his breeding range in a given direction, a species overflowing into new territory, is of historical importance and first-page ornithological news. And if the bird moving in on you happens to be the vermilion flycatcher, there should be a celebration, and plaques of permanent character should be installed to commemorate and mark for all time his first nesting sites. We make greater to-do than this about occurrences of far less importance.

For a really scientific and comprehensive treatment of such movements in this area we shall have to wait until map-series covering many years, showing breeding ranges of various species, have been prepared from accumulated data and made available, basis for which, of course, will be Dr. Harry C. Oberholser's great work on Texas birds, now in manuscript.[1] In the meantime, there is no harm in indulging in speculations concerning specific cases.

The vermilion flycatcher seems to love two physiographic features not often found in conjunction, viz., a desert, or semiarid terrain, contiguous to a body of still water. This condition has been artificially created in many locations during recent years, especially in the Southwest.

In the San Antonio area this flycatcher hugs the shores of Medina Lake. He immediately occupied the semiarid slopes bordering the great lake formed by the completion of the Elephant Butte Dam a short distance north of El Paso. The bird is common on the Gila near Silver City, and on the Mimbres while that deceptive stream still flows aboveground through rather barren mountains. A mile or two back in the pasture from Santa Gertrudis, headquarters of the King Ranch, near Kingsville, Texas, is an artificial lake lying in the midst of semiarid growths of cactus and mesquite. Here are vermilion flycatchers in greater abundance than I have found anywhere else in Texas.

The enormous increase within the past few years of earthen tanks of considerable size and permanent nature is expanding and enriching natural life on the Edwards Plateau. Such artificial reservoirs are no new thing in this semiarid region, but the art of building one that will endure is new. The early settlers simply damned up small streams and arroyos in the hope of holding over a supply of water from the wet winter season. Comparatively few of these attempts were successful. Floods, if they did not sweep away the dams, soon filled the reservoirs with mud. It has taken federal subsidy, government specifications, and a system of government inspection to teach the simple art of building a permanent earthen tank.

It has been found that the selection of a site is a matter of first importance. It must be in the way of enough drainage to fill, and yet not in the path of destructive floods. The excavation must be made in material that will hold water. The dam itself must be built to specifications which engineering experience has demonstrated as necessary to insure permanence. It would seem that a one-page itemization of simple directions would be sufficient to teach the public how to do it. But the public doesn't learn that way. To acquire the art of building an earthen reservoir right, it must have demonstrations and be paid handsomely to accept something for its own benefit. The AAA plan of subsidization in return for the privilege of governmental planning and inspection has been enormously expensive, but it works.

These small ponds, built to specifications, supervised and rigidly inspected before being approved for subsidy payment, present an impressive accumulation, distinguishing the enterprise as a successful governmental experiment in the field of geotechnics.

Within the past five years there have been constructed in Hays County 400 approved reservoirs; in Caldwell County, 550; in Guadalupe County, 650; in Travis County, 700; and so on. In these four counties alone, 2,300 permanent earthen tanks have been built following proper specifications with an average excavation for each tank of about eighteen hundred cubic yards. This development has been duplicated in counties all over the semiarid Edwards Plateau, with what immense implications for increases in wild life it is impossible even to estimate. In the four counties listed, there exist now around 4,000,000 cubic yards of water with aggregate surface area of nearly 800 acres where none existed five years ago. Moreover, these ponds are dotted in strategically for bird life. They are somewhat evenly spaced throughout the area.

I have just observed the filling by pump of one of these reservoirs having a water surface of about a quarter of an acre, and twelve feet deep in the center. The site chosen for it was a gentle depression in an old field which had been worn out and rendered worthless by fifty years of unscientific cultivation. The spot was barren and baked to a crisp in the blazing heat of the July sun. It took about three weeks to fill this reservoir; and from the time when there began to be a sizable puddle of water, life gravitated to it. Minnows were the first manifestation to appear—their eggs must have been sucked through the intake screen; next came water moccasins to devour them; soon numerous dragonflies were zooming back and forth over the surface, evidencing the presence of still smaller insects; certain water skaters came next. When the thing was about half-full, frogs began hopping out of nowhere along the borders, and the doleful killdeer searched the dampened soil at nightfall in advance of the rising water.

Most vocal of all life here assembled, especially in the twilight periods, is the frog. I am tempted to say the most altruistic also, for he seems to make it his business in life to provide other species with succulent tidbits to be gobbled up or squeezed past the narrows of a throat in a leisurely, hours-long process of successive gulpings, depending upon whether it is a heron or a snake which accepts his invitation. There is hardly another form of life which is eaten so freely and with such relish by so many different species. It seems that the frog does not eat to live so much as he lives to be eaten.

Tied by his amphibious nature to a water's-edge habitat—happy hunting ground for both land and water predators—he has been equipped with only a hop-and-hide defense: and his "hop" is not far nor does his "hide" show any genius for concealment. A telltale toe may be left sticking out, or a propped-up leaf or a cloud of rising sediment may advertise his whereabouts. From the approach of a marsh bird, he plunges into the water with a resounding splash which attracts his water enemies to an underwater chase. Becoming short of breath or being routed out by some voracious enemy, he returns to land. Thus he is battered from watery pillow to earthen post, back and forth, hopping, hiding, diving, throughout a precarious existence which usually ends in catastrophe.

One afternoon a distress-croak attracted my attention and, looking about a bit, I found in a patch of weeds near the pond a young frog struggling to free himself from a snake—a dark, olive-green snake with a yellowish stripe down each side and speckled with yellowish dots along the back. His head was small and slender, and the largest diameter of his body was not much greater than that of an ordinary lead pencil. The head and neck were even smaller.

I judged the frog was at least an inch across the shoulders, while the spread of his forelegs added another inch. The hind legs were already swallowed when I arrived, and the upper lip of the snake was feeling along the rump of his victim. The lower jaw was forced back so that the angle made at the juncture of the jaws was about one hundred and fifty degrees.

The frog clawed frantically with his forefeet in the sand, and the snake took advantage of this struggle by backing gradually to increase resistance while the throat worked urgently with a swallowing motion. The reptile braced himself against the small weeds, and the tip of his tail showed a tendency to coil about a weed every now and then for a securer hold, as he exerted a steady backward pull against the forward struggling of his prey. This aided the swallowing process. If the frog had simply relaxed and allowed himself to be pulled and hauled about at will, the snake could not possibly have swallowed him.

With mouth now distended to the absolute limit and the comparatively huge expanse of the frog's body still in front, it seemed to me that the reptile had attempted an impossible task and was in danger of choking himself to death. But he continued to work steadily and with confidence. Gradually the serpent's upper lip edged on up the frog's back and, in the course of half an hour, reached his shoulders. At that point the effort seemed hopeless, since the forelegs were spread and the frog's throat was palpitating violently, showing that he was still alive in spite of the tremendous pressure on the lower part of his body.

Then the snake began stretching his upper lip to one side with strong, lithe action. It was clear that he was attempting to pick up the right foreleg and stuff it down. This required considerable time and a second attempt. He finally tucked the right leg deftly down his throat, but when he shifted the lip to the other side and attempted to get hold of the left leg in the same way, the right leg got free again. He patiently attended to that, his throat all the time alternately bulging and contracting with great vigor. Finally the right leg was again captured, and with less trouble he quickly disposed of the left leg.

This was the crisis of the operation. Slowly the tip of the snake's upper lip came flush with the tip of the frog's nose. Suddenly, after a short gulp and wriggle, the greatly distended mouth came back to normal, and the neck also thinned down to lead-pencil size. As the enormous mouthful passed down, a squeezing process set in which distributed the bulk evenly along about four inches of the central portion of the snake's body. At the moment I was bending closely over him. He pointed his head toward me, lifting about one third of his length upward in a graceful curve, darted his tongue out half a dozen times in quick succession, turned and made off.

Not only do birds, reptiles, and fish feed upon the frog, but one mammal, the coon, is the frog-eating epicure par excellence. The cunning creature will spend the best part of a night lying in wait or probing patiently in watery trash. When the almost human hand of this sly night-prowler finally closes on its prey down in the submerged leaves and sediment, he first kills it delicately with firm and continuous pressure of the "fingers." Then, with the happy flourish of an artist putting the finishing touches to a picture, he washes the lovely morsel in clear surface water and, figuratively pushing back his cuffs and smoothing out his napkin, consumes it in a fashion with which no censor of table manners could find fault.

The frog has little or no brains. The small boy captures a canful for fish bait while you wait. The fable of the frog and the bull has a sound basis in the former's often disastrous overestimate of his own swallowing ability. He is noted the world over for attempting to ingest objects much too large. A sizable frog can make away with a hummingbird or a duckling, but he is not always content with small fry. My friend, Professor Milton R. Gutsch, reports seeing a duck disappear mysteriously from the surface of the pond. Upon fishing him out, he found the duck's head lodged in the belly of a bullfrog. He pulled the frog off, as he would a glove, and released the bird still alive and little the worse for the experience.

Considering the frog's wide popularity as an article of diet, his own poor judgment in attacking his prey, his lack of defensive weapons, his ill-advised vocalism, and his general stupidity, it is a marvel that he survives at all. But, as is the case with so many defenseless and dull-witted forms of life, an enormous fecundity coupled with considerable protective coloration comes to the rescue of this tailless amphibian which, with its one hundred and fifty American species alone, occupies a secure position.

As night closes in about this new pond the frogs croak out a call that may be heard a good mile away. How many mouths water at the sound, and how many forms edge nearer in the gathering darkness, stealthily swimming, crawling, or treading noiselessly the oozy margins—all converging upon the hospitable chorus in a rivalry silent but intense, for the favor or the flavor of the croakers! Thus, offering himself as an award, the frog attracts a new and various night life to the pond.

Meantime, as these accommodating creatures call in night rovers, whose eyes gather strange luster from the gathering darkness, and while the faintest glow is still visible in the western sky, day-flying insects give place to those which night now teases out of hiding. Feeding upon them a solitary bat circles round and round over the pond. Awkwardly pumping, seeking his prey in nervous, erratic darts and dashes, what a travesty this mammal makes of flight! Thus the great business of eating and of being eaten goes on, night and day, underwater, on the surface, and in the upper air, twenty-four hours, right around the clock.

Morning brings two phoebes and a prospecting martin to find out whether the day-flying insects have yet arrived; a dozen doves come in for water; lark sparrows flutter down for a drink and a bath; a spotted sandpiper makes a complete circuit, teetering along, gathering a rich harvest; and an American egret courses in, flying majestically from the direction of the rising sun, takes two turns over the pond, high in the air, and returns eastward.

So, by the time the water had risen to the spillway, a cluster of living forms had already begun to gather, smoothly functioning and ready to receive constant accessions until every nook and cranny, hole, channel, or minute interstice of this many-chambered mansion would be crowded with life flowing in with the water.

Much of this life is new, an accretion, in the sense that it is life which would not have existed at all except for the opportunity thus created. What an ecological revolution has been set in motion by the introduction of water into this spot of desert soil! Plant life is yet to come, and its coming will effect a still profounder revolution and present a further extension of the opportunity for life in one form or another. Numerous species will find each its nook or niche in this artificial structure. And one niche, I think, is reserved for the bird I have been talking about, the vermilion flycatcher, especially around ponds which, like this one, happen to be in open spaces located on the more elevated terraces.

Thus I come to the conclusion that the New Deal has brought to the Edwards Plateau, among other things good and bad, the vermilion fly-catcher by providing the two conditions which this bird seems to demand: one, a rather open, semiarid country; and, two, spaces of still water.

The first condition was created by subsidizing cedar-cutting. Under the stimulus of this subsidy, great spaces have been opened in the thickest cedar brakes, leaving growths of cactus, mesquite, scrub oak, and various shrubs intact. But this alone is not enough.

Then came the dam-building enterprises by which the Colorado River has now a string of lakes beginning at Austin and extending for two hundred miles up its course. As these lakes filled, water encroached on semiarid hillsides cleared of cedar, thus offering a hospitable habitat for the Mexican migrant.

Finally, the earthen tanks are now spaced somewhat evenly over hundreds of square miles, some serving as way stations and others as seasonable abodes. This gorgeous southern flycatcher will follow up the lake shores in the semiarid country as far as the lakes extend, and at the same time he will find pond sites here and there which exactly suit him. There seems to be no reason why he will not penetrate farther north to similar lakes on the Brazos River, certainly to the shores of the one made in semiarid hills by the 'Possum Kingdom Dam.

---

[1] Editor's note: Harry Olberholser, *The Bird Life of Texas*, ed. by Edgar Kincaid, John Rowlett, and Suzanne Winckler (Austin: University of Texas Press, 1974). Olberholser died in 1963, and the manuscript was edited posthumously.

Clear Creek, David Taylor

CHAPTER 2

JOHN GRAVES

KINDRED SPIRITS

John Graves lives near Glen Rose, Texas, on his four-hundred-acre farm. He is the author of several books; among them are *Goodbye to a River* (1960), *Hardscrabble* (1974), *From a Limestone Ledge* (1977), and his recent memoir *Myself and Strangers* (2004). "Kindred Spirits" is taken from *From a Limestone Ledge*.

I have what started out as a canvas-covered wooden canoe, though with the years it has taken on some aluminum in the form of splinting along three or four fractured ribs, and this past spring I replaced its rotting cloth rind with resin-impregnated fiberglass. It is thus no longer the purely organic piece of handicraft that emerged from a workshop in Maine some decades back. Nor do I use it more than occasionally these days, to run a day's stretch of pretty river or just to get where fish may be. Nevertheless I retain much fondness for it as a relic of a younger, looser, less settled time of life.

While readying its hull for the fiberglass I had to go over it inch by inch as it sat on sawhorses in the barn—removing the mahogany outwales and stripping off the old canvas, locating unevennesses in the surface of the thin cedar planking, sanding and filling and sanding again so that protuberances and pits would not mar the new shell or lessen its adhesion, and finally taking out the seats and thwarts and readying the interior for fresh varnish. The process took up a good bit of my spare time for weeks, and during it I got to know a couple of Indians fairly well. At least I thought of them as Indians, for the canoe company which takes its name from the

Old Town of the Penobscots used to employ many of that tribe's members as workers, and for all I know still does.

There was the Good Indian, as I came to call him, who had stood on the left side of the craft while it was being built ("port" and "starboard" will not serve, for the thing had lain sometimes rightside up on its trestle or table or whatever had held it, and sometimes upside down), selecting and trimming his planks with care and affixing them to the ribs so that their edges and butts fitted tightly and the tracks were driven precisely flush, drilling his screw and bolt holes true. And across from him on the right side had labored his confrere Slovenly Pete, a brooder and a swigger of strong waters during the long Maine winter nights, who with reddened eye and palsied hand had messed up everything he could without getting fired from his job. Their ghosts were with me, and I spoke to them as I went over their work and did my own. The Good Indian was a friend, a taciturn perfectionist in sympathy with my resolve to get things right. But somehow I took more interest in his shiftless mate, a sour and gabby type who responded to my gibes about hammer marks and ill-matched planks and protruding tackheads with irrelevant rhetoric on white men's viperish ways, or biting queries as to what business a Texan had fretting over a canoe in the first place. "Your God damn rivers," he said at one point, "ain't got no God damn water in them most of the God damn time."

I've been in this sort of touch with many artisans and laborers over the years, for I am both a putterer and a countryman, categories of humanity that frequently busy themselves in refurbishing and repairing things that other human beings have made or refurbished or repaired in times gone by, leaving personal imprints on them. An old Ford tractor, for example, whose hydraulic pump was replaced by a previous owner with a second one from another model, by dint of much ingenious grinding and shimming and drilling, can cause one to ponder and blaspheme for days over the question of why the costly new pump he has driven fifty miles to buy at a dealership can't be seated. And if, when starting casually to pull out a decayed forty-year-old cornerpost set four feet deep, in order to put a new one in its place, you discover that whoever installed it was such a fence nut that he filled the hole around it with angular crushed road gravel tamped down to grip like death, your emotions are mixed as you strive without success to budge his monument with a tractor drawbar or a jack rated to five thousand pounds' lift. On the one hand you have to admire the uncompromising correctness that made him go to such trouble; on the other, more strongly, you wish that in the matter of fence strength he had been a bit more of a slob, like yourself.

Sweatily romantic couples who have redone, maybe rebuilt, old houses with their own hands, ripping out ancient wallpaper and linoleum and pipes and wiring and such, searching out pockets of dry rot and settled foundation piers and chimney cracks, working everything down to bare wood and masonry or beyond, nearly always arrive at intimacy with their predecessors in those abodes, their Good Indians and Slovenly Petes. Nearly always too they find the villains more interesting than the nice guys. It is, of course, most pleasant to learn that underneath some textoned plasterboard and eight or ten layers of bargain-basement latex paint and wallpaper and white lead and alligatored varnish and the like, you're the owner of a room paneled in wave-grained solid black walnut beautifully fitted and jointed, or that above the rusty stamped-tin ceilings of a stone Hill Country cabin are beams of native post oak hewn square with an adze by some ancestral Deutscher. But it's probably a bit more fascinating to discover, as a friend of mine did, that the faint stink which has seeped for years from a north kitchen wall and has lately grown too stout to ignore derives from the grassroots inventive genius of an anonymous former occupant who insulated that wall by filling its stud spaces with cottonseed hulls, fermented now by a siding leak into rich and miasmic silage.

One has to face also from time to time some effect or the other of the powerful belief, among Prairie Gothic carpenters of a more innocent era, that a two-by-four would serve for just about any purpose. I've seen whole upper floors sustained by joists of those dimensions, a bit concave and springy underfoot but still functional, and in one antiquated farmhouse that my wife and I rented cheaply several years because we were willing to refinish it ourselves, I traced some mysterious cracks and sags to a small bracket built out of five or six short lengths of two-by-four yellow pine nailed halfway up the wall of a closet and sheathed in shiplap. It held up an entire brick woodstove flue that must have weighed, according to my rough computation, about 4500 pounds avoirdupois. I had strange feelings about that chimney and the ghost who'd put it there, and I hoped that whenever it fell it would choose to collapse straight down toward where its foundation ought to have been, rather than topple sideways through the attic and ceiling onto the bed where gentle sleep enveloped us or the table where we ate. But now, nine years after we moved out of that house and maybe sixty or seventy after the chimney was erected, I note with interest whenever I drive along that road that it is still poking up quite vertically above the roofline, and in fact wintertime wisps of smoke tell me that a current tenant enamored of alternative energy has hooked up a woodstove to it again.

Living now on this place we have owned for two decades where I built all the structures, sometimes with help but often not, the ghost I most usually have to confront is myself. A chimney that leaks at its flashings, an outbuilding set up on blocks of wood through which termites have made a gleeful invasion, a sheet-iron barn roof that siphons rainwater at some seams when certain winds are blowing, a crawl-space inundated by storms through the place where waterpipes enter—all these joys and others are traceable not to the faulty theories or sloppiness of old-time carpenters and masons but to my own apprentice ignorance. An owner-builder lives with his botches, and working to correct them he waxes introspective, not necessarily with admiration.

I seldom work up the guts for that ultimate form of puttering which involves that patching or restoration of good antique furniture and other classic artifacts. Stout, relatively crude, country-made relics, whose charm is in their honesty and in the sheen of long hard use, I will tackle willingly enough, for the stout crude honest repairs that befit them are within my capacity and their native woods and other materials are usually easy to match. But it takes naïveté or a special sort of arrogance to tamper with the civilized products of vanished masters' vanished dexterity with hand tools. Their aged and chip-prone hardwoods, harvested perhaps in distant forests of the old British Empire where tigers burned bright and white men carried a metaphoric burden and dark men a literal one, are very hard to duplicate with inserts or patches made from woods available now. Furthermore the powered machines on which most present woodworkers depend won't reproduce the contours of their moldings and furbelows, and authenticity prohibits the use of epoxies and other miracle fillers and cements, mainstay substances in modern repair. Bungled work can lower their often considerable value, so like most other people I'm usually willing to leave restoration to professionals or to let the wounded things sit in their corners as is.

Spirits inhabit them too, of course, those of their gifted makers in the individual organic perfection of their shaping and joining and decoration, those of intermediate Slovenly Petes in crude repair jobs undertaken at some point in their history and showing up now as ill-seated reinforcement blocks and screwdriver nicks and other defects. And if one does let arrogance tempt him into essaying such a job himself, as I have on rare occasions, more often than not he ends up leaving a Slovenly Pete spoor also, or else giving up in the middle and either abandoning the object in question in a dismantled state or letting somebody else puzzle it back together. Sometimes with a flash of guilt I run across envelopes or cartons with labels on them in my own handwriting such as "Trim from dressing room bureau" or "Pieces of rosewood snuffbox." This latter project hit a dead end some eleven years ago when I was unable to find any nickel silver of the right thickness for making a new delicate hinge to replace a broken one, and then it got forgotten in a round of very different puttering, the framing of a barn. I do still intend to seek out that metal and finish up the job, though, maybe in tremulous old age when my chances of being a Slovenly Pete will be even better than now.

In addition to being a putterer with things, I find with some surprise, having spent much of my younger life avoiding ownership when I could, that I have turned into a hoarder of them too. Marriage and parenthood are partly to blame, I guess, and country life even more. At any rate the owned objects that surround us now—some still serving a good purpose, some serving none at all, others awaiting a time of use or donation to somebody else—form massive clutters in workshop and office, and pile up in attics and on platforms under the barn roof and in any odd corner of our house and outbuildings that stays unoccupied for more than a week or so. I do sometimes muse out pleasurable fantasies of setting some large fires or holding a huge garage sale and then driving away with my mate to a spare life aboard a small ketch in coastal waters, but the fact is that I seem to be stuck with these belongings in a complex way. They *belong* where they are just about as much as I do, and if some morning I were to walk into the barn and note that an accustomed item was not there—say the battered Rube Goldberg seed cleaner that I picked up at a farm auction and use maybe once in three years, between which times it sits there stolidly collecting mud-dauber nests and goat-manure dust and blocking passage—I would feel my little world's foundations shudder slightly.

Undoubtedly the main trouble is that nearly all these impedimenta have spirits in them by now, either for me or my wife and daughters or simply themselves. They were made by somebody, even if that somebody was only a stamping-machine jockey in some dark satanic mill of Pittsburgh or Chicopee Falls. Most bear marks of human use and misuse, and some, of the sort one starts accumulating as older relatives die off and one becomes an older relative oneself, have family stories and meanings attached to them. Heavy tables and sets of shelves put together by my late father, an inveterate putterer himself, tools and World War I stuff of his, a great-grandfather's gargoyled notary seal, large brass-latched Bibles with genealogical scribblings that omit most data about miscreants and black sheep, the cow's-horn cup that Great Uncle Billy Cavitt whittled out for his little sister, my grandmother, as he lay in a tent hospital getting used to the absence of a leg shot off at Pleasant Hill, the thirty-two that Grandpa bought for defense against a gambler in Cuero after a horsewhipping in which Grandpa had wielded the whip…

Others recapitulate past bits of my own existence and if, as has been claimed, the unexamined life is not worth living, I suppose they serve a useful end. Certainly if one has made a good many haphazard changes of direction in his lifetime it is at least instructive every now and then, after a certain point, to catch a glimpse of something that one was before. The Old Town canoe carries freight like that, along with its spectral red crew. An earring from an early love's rosy lobe can still rowel memory, as can things like a Boy Scout hatchet, still good, a set of blackened silver lieutenant's bars, or a curious brass halyard snap given me long ago by a

sailing friend in Mallorca and used now as a paperweight. A volume of
James Branch Cabell, encountered lately in rummaging, made me pause
and wonder over the very young me who admired and imitated his work,
thank God without publishing the results, and a moth-tattered collection of trout flies that I tied up myself nearly thirty years ago, nymphs
and wet flies and dries in all manner of patterns and sizes, brought back
with freshness a compressed and separate parenthesis of time spent in
a high valley of the Sangre de Cristo. I lived there alone for six months
in a spruce-log shack rented from a rancher-Penitente, wrote earnest
confused stories about the war, went down to Santa Fe for supplies and
carousel when I felt like it or needed to, and with absorption fished the
pools and riffles of a crystal alder-shaded creek either by myself or with
an old and close and troublesome friend who would drive up from
Albuquerque on weekends. Except that one Friday night he made a few
bars before setting out and two o'clock in the morning his car flipped
over in the desert near a place called Galisteo and that was all of that, but
I and the moth-gnawed Royal Coachmen and Bivisibles remain.

Freight enough … Despite everything, there does still dwell in me a
remnant of that fellow who didn't want to own things, and for sanity on
occasion I'm glad to know he's there. Sometimes he rears up and asserts
himself and I muster the nerve to throw out a few cartons and sacks and
pickup loads of unusable gear, or give them away, or burn them. But then
the spirits start squeaking and gibbering in rage (ours do seem to make
such noises, like Elizabethan spirits: not for them the quavering moan of
midnight grade C movies) and I stay my hand before matters go too far.
For it is well known among devotees of the occult that offended spirits
are much less easy to live with than unoffended ones. And if one lives
in a world dominated by things, how shall he know what spirits lurk
where?

Rio Grande, Carol Cullar

CHAPTER 3

CAROL CULLAR

12 VARIATIONS ON A THEME OR WHY I LIVE IN SOUTHWEST TEXAS

Carol Cullar is Executive Director of the Rio Bravo Nature Center Foundation, Inc. in Eagle Pass, Texas. She holds the Rio Grande and its preservation/conservation dear to her heart. Both visual artist and writer, her most recent book, *Maverick in the Chaparral: the Eagle Pass Poems*, focuses on living on La Frontera and 26 years in the Tamaulipan Biotic Province of Southwest Texas. The great-granddaughter of Robert Wilmeth Crossman (poet, inventor, nephew and namesake of the R. W. Crossman who died in the Alamo, US Marshall of the Oklahoma Territory, and cohort of Wyatt Earp), Cullar credits her ancestor's frontier spirit with her restless dissatisfaction with civilization and her determination to live on the Frontera in Southwest Texas—or it could be pure-dee cussedness that has given her a love of Maverick County. Cullar's Texas roots run deep, but as a young woman, she took afternoon tea with Generalissimo de Santa Ana's granddaughter and considers the dispute settled.

A few years back, I'd just finished installing the wood stove in the studio here on the Rio Grande, when my mother gave me her old teakettle, the one she'd started married life with back before the Second World War.

The relic added a whimsical touch to the rustic stove, and I planned to fill it to provide needed moisture to the heated air of my inaugural fire. As the first splash of water hit the dusty kettle's bottom, a pungent aroma sprang up, claiming my senses in one staggering assault. I was enveloped by the odor, thrown back to Western Oklahoma from whence the family roots diverge, where the sandy road threaded across the railroad tracks, south to my grandfather's farm, where the pear sprang tall by the path to the barnyard, where the earth wrapped us in cotton patches and shelterbelts, far-stretching milo fields, and fresh-mowed sorghum.

A few months later on a trip to Michoacan, I mentioned to a fellow monarch enthusiast my powerful response to that encapsulated odor of my birthplace and learned from her that the French have long known the potent strength of the earth's essence, given it a name—*terroir*.

What if there were an essential homeplace stitched up in the fibers of our being, locked in our sinews and the molecules of our synapses? Is it only country kids who grew up on the back of a dusty tractor who feel this tie to the earth? Must we have run barefoot a thousand miles through the soil of our youth to pattern that scent into our nature? If we drank the rainwater and the cistern water, bathed in the pumpings from the well, are our molecules not bound together with the rivers and the streams, the vegetables from the garden and the honey garnered from a million blooms?

Thus, what brought me here to this ramshackle place on the banks of the Rio Grande a quarter-century ago is irrelevant, but what holds me here is everything. The limestone deposit that lines the new electric teakettle is as much a part of the calcium in my bones as is the pollen in the local huisache honey an integral component of my flesh.

And so when the taciturn folks scattered through this threnody of thorns that is the Tamaulipan Biotic Province and Southwest Texas respond to the query of why we have stuck it out here, put down such deep roots, our likely response is, "Well, it grows on ya."

During those last twenty-six years of my bones' slow transubstantiation from restless wanderings over most of the continent to the same calcium carbonate bedrock of Southwest Texas' ancient seabeds, I have journaled in my attempt to capture Maverick County's *terroir* and my bondedness with it. What follows are twelve of those meanderings:

To stand amid: immersed in scent of roses beneath the double-helixed coil of forty buzzards sporting *en plein aire*, is to know one's self a step upwind of death and mortal to the bone.

I know these hills—I've drawn their buttes for many a year. Those scarps are stored in the muscles of my fingers, the bones of my wrists. Bone-stored hills, buttes; and in my hand, muscled limestone. In ochre paths, my thighs, making sense of things, tacking it to something of my own, I draw the arroyos, the juniper and yucca, springtime's green, dust of summer, or fall of snow. These hills are mine—their buttes my bones, their faults—my feet of clay.

Spring settled onto the desert like a fat woman lowering huge, soft buttocks onto the brittle webbing of last year's lawnchair—uncertainty in every quivering descent; refusing to trust her full weight—first testing winter's field-dressed thorns—an inconspicuous blossom or two on very short stems, of course, then a settling of palest chartreuse over the mesquite. Her intent is clear, her course inexorable, but her hope is to distribute her vast girth over the land with equal economies of motion and passion, with strength to spare in the event her intended target might not be ready for a full onslaught—and an emergency pull-up might be necessary rather than a three point landing to full-stop. But once settled, Spring is well situated, refusing to budge until the sweltering sun of summer sends her further north with the imprint of the chaparral's prickly webbing stamped in the flesh of her rounded thighs. Majestic, she sweeps toward the plateaus and prairies, the pillowed rests of the northern states—and leaves the desert of the Southwest—a broken lawnchair in the dust of summer.

How could I write of snow, tell of cold and silent purity in this place? Here, where each agent conspires to thwart its coming, where the earth is a tan biscuit steaming, and the river's waters leak slowly down beefy sides like thin brown gravy? Where is the place for snow in such fractaled chaos of burning dust? This debauched Virgin reeling as she stumbles her long way home need never fear the frozen ditch; this hot-thighed bride garbed in dark mesquite will never wear its whiteness to her marriage bed, nor will all enveloping forgiveness grace this brown Jesus. They have assured their resurrection by other means and will not be touched by cold white fingers. How could I write of snow?

A maverick pulse: we tell each other tales of wildness of panthers in the *monte* (countryside) at ease beside the narrow road as we were passing by. It pleases us—the isolation, the mavericks in the chaparral, the certain knowledge of the closeness of the untamed edge of things. We mention how the desert air speaks of distances thrown open to the limitless expanse of sky and whispers hotly through the dusk of yet another fiery eve. While nostrils flare in primal reflex to catch the scent of dusty bloom, our ears attune to life's caesura and pulses subtly alter to fit a desert pace. El Indio on the Rio Grande is song and cadence of a bygone drum that thrums an autochthonal heartbeat through the canebrakes by the river and twines us in her untamed meter, till we know that panthers come. So we choose to live in desert places and tell each other tales of wildness, thereby taking to ourselves a measure of that primeval essence which pulls us near untrammeled, untamed edges of the world.

Punto final: this book of bones was but a brief history, white pages scattered midst chaparral. Femur and tibia gnawed in ultimate punctuation by coyote and *zopilote* (buzzard) to rate a single codicil in the local weekly news: "*… the skeletal remains of an unidentified illegal alien were found today on the Flores Ranch.*" Undaunted by two hundred miles of rolling guajillo, huisache, mesquite, and cactus stretched eternally in a haze of heat, they write their brief passage in sand and reach alone their destination, never knowing that no boundary, fence, nor spoken word of law or legislation has ever stopped the flow of man, a people in migration—yet ranchers find their bones: brief pages torn from our history lesson.

Yellow dogs bark from the hillside, past the wind, beyond reason and hope.

Beneath a darkling sunset desert lightning seen afar, intermittent portent of what comes this way at dawn. No Bethlehem this, but a Gomorrah—or Gethsemane—set down by one dark river; and flotsam on the current that sucks round all the pilings gets pushed up on this shore. A Sargasso of intentions where stoutest timbers rot—some are ferruginously drawn here between forces poles apart. The twisted tree—it grows here—and whatsoever of its ilk: the thorn, the asp, the rose—in Armageddon-put-on-hold.

It is the passage that I love between the shoals and reefs that lurk in seeming innocence, but like a Dali painting conceal another image if one looks from altered eyes, while timeless sirens sing amid the rocks, and Scylla and Charybdis wait. On either side, the hovels molder; peasants barter balding tires and wilting fruit in ramshackle booths beneath scraggly trees; but it is the passage that I love—between ideologies and cultures unfamiliar, rich, piquant— alien and unexpected as an armchair abandoned by the road, inviting, comfortable, but implying wrongness by its very place-ment. Dusky hands entreat, reach, cling in mist and smoke from the metal salvage yard. Acrid smell of human ammonia and Mr. B's barbecue grope for our senses as we rush past, windows closed, eyes averted, goals intent before us. We tell our beads, kiss the thumb for the Lady of Lourdes, lest we are lured to either side; but it is the passage that I love.

Fires across the vega, smoky pillars rise miles away. From the vantage of my hill, two, sometimes three, are visible beyond the river of division half a world away. Distance has obscured the flames, but telltale grayness columns upward, reaches colder strata, turns abruptly north northwest. What is burning in the distance—in foreign lands so close? Do the totems guide through some wilder-ness wanderers—will there be flames by night? We have no such bright blazes behind our barriers—legislated, regulated—we have no inexplicable burnings, but between that third world and the first must limp this second.

Sanctuary: If that distant gilded spire glimpsed between straggled mesquites were not the beef feedlot, were instead some far cathe-dral's awkward reach toward grandeur; and if the grey eminence of *Los Cerritos del Burro,* The Little Donkey Peaks, were not reduced to a sketched silhouette along the western world-rim by sixty miles of desert monody; and if this scrawny chaparral tangled out across those flats and gullies, thatched and prickled by an infinity of thorns, wiry as the *mons veneris* of an aged whore, were not *de vez en cuando* (from time to time) painted with a thousand hues, embroidered with the rare incense of sanctuary; then this earth, this dry and dusty place, this desert tabernacle would not compel my pagan heart, nor lift my jaded eye to boundless principalities: and I, voluptuary at the sapphire shrine.

I have caught the wind that whistles through the buzzard-stripped carcass of all my fleshless dreams; I cannot let it go.

Oak Tree, David Taylor

CHAPTER 4

PETE GUNTER

A SENSE OF ONE PLACE AS THE FOCUS OF ANOTHER: THE MAKING OF A CONSERVATIONIST

Pete A. Y. Gunter is past president of the Big Thicket Association and currently serves as Big Thicket Task Force Chairman of the Texas Committee on Natural Resources. He grew up in Houston and Gainesville and has divided his time between writing on environmental issues, teaching philosophy, and writing about the relationship between philosophy and environmental ethics. Among the products of this latter preoccupation are *Texas Land Ethics* (1997) with Max Oelschlaeger, plus numerous articles and reviews.

I have been haunted, while writing this paper, by Annie Dillard's remarks concerning human perception in *Pilgrim at Tinker Creek*. We see the world impressionistically, she admonishes, noting the green fringe of trees, the blue sky, a swatch of grass, a few human figures in the foreground or background. We feel at home in a world which we have constituted for ourselves out of a mixture of impressionistic gloss and sheer familiarity:

> We don't know what's going on here. If these tremendous events are random combinations of matter run amok, the

yield of millions of monkeys at millions of typewriters, then what is it in us, hammered out of these same typewriters, that they ignite? We don't know. Our life is a faint tracing on the surface of mystery, like the idle, curved tunnels of leaf miners on the face of a leaf. We must somehow take a wider view, look at the whole landscape, really see it, and describe what's going on here. Then at least we can wail the right question into the swaddling band of darkness, or, if it comes to that, choir the proper praise.

That is how environmentalism began for me. I didn't know what was going on, in nature or in environmentalism. I discovered the hard way, through experience.

How wonderfully naïve I was, with an undifferentiated, fulsome love of nature and a political optimism straight out of Perry Mason and the Boy Scout Creed. I not only believed that Justice Would Triumph; I believed that Ordinary Citizens, by luck, pluck, and native deviousness, could band together and defeat Goliath: lumber Goliath, big wealth Goliath, political Goliath.

I believed all that. But this was in 1960, when Hubert Humphrey lived. Then there was *Hope*. Not very intelligent hope, but *Hope*.

I remember, as a graduate student in the north, finding a volume in the university bookstore titled *I'll Take Texas* by Mary Lasswell. As I recall, it was in puce and magenta. I hid it in a plain brown wrapper, sneaked it to my room where, late at night, behind locked doors, I read it. A chapter on the coming demise of the once sprawling Big Thicket stuck in my craw. (Ivy League people are not supposed to have craws, but after all, I was only a graduate student, not a real Yalie.) I managed to build up my courage and write a letter to newly elected Senator Ralph W. Yarborough (D.-Tex.) urging that at least part of the Big Thicket be set aside for future generations. Save the Everglades of Texas, I wrote. Save the Big Thicket!

The big what? The Big Thicket, a wilderness/semiwilderness in Southeast Texas. On a map you would find it northwest of Beaumont and northeast of Houston: from thirty to eighty miles from the Gulf Coast. As a boy I fished and hunted there with a friend who had relatives in the area.

True sons of Texas, my buddy and I were a menace then to anything that moved and most things that didn't. I possessed only a single shot Winchester .22 rifle. But with that rifle and ten boxes of hollow point, long rifle shells, I could, and did, decimate whole populations of hawks, woodpeckers, snakes, chickens, armadillos, and even an occasional squirrel. In those days, we knew what it was like to be a real Man.

As it turns out, the Thicket is a kind of ecological ark, possessing great biological diversity. Dry sandlands and sphagnum bogs, coastal prairies and river floodplain forests, rolling piney hills and palmetto flats, baygalls, seeps, fern valleys, live there cheek by jowl in great profusion, supporting tropical, temperate, eastern and western vegetation, birds, insect life: A thousand varieties of flowering plants. Over thirty species of ferns and as many of orchids. Four species of insectivores. Though the Big Thicket once covered over three million-plus acres, timbering, towns, roads, dams, oil fields, and oil pipelines had reduced the Thicket to around 400,000 acres by the time I happened onto it with my lethal .22.

But to reiterate:

I knew about none of this. At most, I realized its folklore: old stories of escapees from the state penitentiary at Huntsville running for the

Thicket ahead of the baying hounds, of people still living in back places in log cabins with coal oil lanterns, of Confederate deserters hiding out by the sloughs and backwaters safe from conscription officers—and from Shiloh, Chicamauga, Vicksburg. Of bear hunts. Of treed raccoons on moonbright October nights.

Yes, it was hard to miss the folklore.

Only, I didn't know to call it that.

But to return to activism. To my amazement Senator Yarborough wrote back: not only wrote back but announced that because of a newly passed law he was able to set aside wilderness in Texas' national forests. He informed me that approximately 2000 acres of Big Thicket vegetation were being set aside by his request in the Sam Houston National Forest and urged me to go immediately to Texas and meet several high national forest officials who would be writing to me. They would take me on a special tour of the Big Thicket.

You could have knocked me over with a pine needle. What could I say to those foresters? How could I distinguish the Big Thicket vegetation the chief forester referred to in his letter from any other kind of vegetation? Forests looked much alike to me; so, beyond a minimal commonsense knowledge, did trees. I'd know a bear if I saw one. But the forester didn't mention bears. Besides, they were now extinct in East Texas.

So I ducked the senator's suggestion and the Chief Forester's invitation and went out to get an environmental education instead. One of those people mentioned in Mary Lasswells' book was Lance Rosier, a home-grown conservationist from Saratoga, Texas, who had spent years leading writers, scientists, and garden clubs into the Big Thicket. On the way back from the north to Texas, I stopped in at Saratoga and befriended Lance, and followed him around Pine Island, and Bayou, and Village Creek and Wildcat Slough, writing down in a small spiral notebook whatever he could tell me—plenty, more than I could grasp—about the Thicket, past and present. About orchids, and resurrection ferns, and the lore of backwoodsmen, and hawks, and spiders, and a thousand other things. A couple of dozen lessons with Lance, on trips between graduate school and Houston and back left me stuffed with data, fogged with folklore, and determined to do what I could. For Lance had seen the wilderness receding, fading, needlessly dying. And he said so.

It was then that I began as a writer: first with reviews and short articles in *The Living Wilderness, Florida Naturalist, Kountze News, Texas Observer*—whoever would publish. In due time I joined the newly founded Big Thicket Association, began attending meetings, became involved in projects, and finally, ended up—to my considerable amazement—struggling to lead a statewide and finally national crusade to save the Big Thicket.

A real environmental campaign is exhausting and confusing. If there ever were an example of William James' "blooming budding confusion," this is it. With much help from many friends, I was to give over 200 speeches and more interviews than I could count and to make dozens of media appearances. The frenetic activity stretched from the *Today Show* to the Pilot Point Kiwanis Club, from the Houston Philosophical Society to the Corsicana Junior High School Assembly Program. Petitions, boycotts, hearings, dinners with politicos, letters, trail rides, barbecues, arguments with lumber public relations men, helicopter rides with cameramen.

You get the picture.

But, really, I did not get it. I really didn't understand myself. Why should an ordinary kid out of Houston, raised like everyone else to do the stuff everyone was supposed to do—play football, make money—turn instead, like Lance, to trying to save Mother Nature. In Saratoga and all around it, in swamps and baygalls, and mixed pine-hardwood forests there was nature worth saving. If there was nature worth saving in Houston, it was quickly being reduced to square suburban lots.

The question still puzzles me today, forty years later. But as I look back on it, it begins to be answered. Before the Big Thicket there was something and somewhere else in my life, which shaped my attitudes: another and different place, threatened in a very different way. It was in my blood, that place—or rather, had been put there irreversibly, long before—a sense of place preceding another sense of place.

I recall, vividly, standing at the front door of my grandparents' house in Gainesville, Texas, nose pressed to the screen. Dad was out on the sidewalk putting his fishing gear in the rumble seat of A. W. Noble's Model A Coupe. Dad waved, climbed in and the car turned away, headed north to the Red River and the camp under White's Bluff. I tried to reach up to the screen door latch, but it was too high. Dad had gone to the promised land and left me there, listening to the tinny drone of the Fort Worth livestock quotations on Grandpa's radio, watching butterfly moths dance around Granny's dried-out rose bushes. "Damn," I said. "Damn."

If Dad kept me in prison that summer in Gainesville, he was soon to set me free. From the time I was six 'til I was grown, every August (and more often, if we could) we would head to the Red River, camping out two or three weeks, fishing, hunting, playing pitch and poker with Dad's old friends and Mom's cousins—whoever felt like joining us.

At sundown, we seined bait and then set our trotlines. After sundown, we would run the lines, after sitting out on a sandbar giving the catfish a chance to bite as the moon rose and the stars wheeled west.

It was then that the folklore—our folklore—settled in. Most of what follows will be that folklore, woven out of stories, the fabric of which determined why I ended up trying to conserve nature, while so many in my generation could not even conceive of doing so. There were hundreds of stories. I can only recount a few of them here. The Gunters had come to that valley shortly after the Civil War, run out of East Texas, the story went, by piney woods boys who didn't appreciate the fine job Captain Gunter did as tithe gatherer and draft officer in Wood County after he barely survived a wound achieved at the Siege of Corinth, up in north Mississippi. The land that they came to after the war was bounded on three sides by Indian Territory, and not a lot safer than the piney woods country they had so abruptly left. For the first decade, they managed to ward off Comanche and Kiowa raids. They had forted up their house, cutting the bottom-land timbers, lopping off their limbs, and driving the tree trunks into the ground topwise, to make a stockade big enough to hold them and some neighbors—the ones willing to stay there. When the Indians were finally imprisoned, at Fort Sill, up in the Territory, the Gunters began raising corn to feed them. The Comanches, ever ungrateful, continued to break out and raid the river bottoms until around 1890.

That kind of world, remote, nearly self-sufficient, was what Dad wanted me to inherit. The Gunters, Giddens, and Ligons were readers, learning what they could about literature and history. But they had to face up to the world around them. With time the harshness of that world receded out of memory. Instead, they recalled a world of coon hunts on chill November nights, of catfish fries and cotton harvests, of owls calling back and forth across the river, of peach orchards and native pecan forests, of raw northers and summer droughts, of vast, sudden floods pushing the river a mile wide. All the stories that were told about it were a kind of glue, binding us to that past, and that world.

If the stories were about animals, they bound you to the animals. If they were about land, or weather, or Indians, they tangled you up in threads of rain, or Indians, or wilderness. Take panthers. By the time I arrived, they were gone; but they managed to live on in countless narratives. One fall, Grandpa told, when he was a boy, he went to a hog killing—a social event and a way of getting meat for winter. For his labors, he was given a tow sack full of pork chops, which he tied to his saddle horn. About half way home, his horse got "skittish," nearly bucking him off. That could happen if a panther were around. So Grandpa took out a pork chop, tossed it into the brush, and spurred the horse into a trot. A mile later, as he crossed a dry creek, the horse bucked again. Grandpa looked back: a panther's upright tail followed like a periscope through tall, yellowed grass. He untied the tow sack, tossed it high in the air, and spurred the horse, arriving home as the sun fell.

Grandpa told that story as a joke on himself. Dad told a similar story of a bunch of kids and a straggle of dogs out hunting raccoons on a moonlit night. The dogs treed an animal in a big pecan tree, and the kids lit smoky fire under it. Dogs barked frantically scrambling up the tree trunk, and the kids shouted and threw rocks. The creature, whatever it was, didn't like the uproar. It jumped and landed right in the middle of the fire, slinging sparks, sticks, and burning leaves. With one lunge the animal bolted into the brush. Boys and dogs also departed, screaming.

Dad said that his brother had brought along a bike that night with big balloon tires, tires that he had deflated but that, even so, could not be ridden in the soft sand. Somehow, Dad pondered, Bud managed to make it back to the house ahead of everyone else, flat tires and all.

No one ever saw what the creature was. But it had to be pretty big to have scattered all that burning brush. And a dozen kids.

Finally—to punctuate the panther stories—Granny had cooked meat pies and put them on a windowsill to cool. She came back later and peered out. A panther stared back at her, its front paws up on the house siding. For a long time, they meditated together, eye to eye. Then the panther dropped down on all fours and padded off into the woods.

It was hard, hearing those stories, to treat a panther as a sworn enemy, red in tooth and claw. No creature curious about meat pies can be all bad. And what creature wouldn't jump if flaming sticks and rocks were thrown at it?

Alongside critter stories there were stories about the river, stories always close relative to the weather. The Red River, it turned out, was as inconsistent in its behavior as many of the people who lived along it. Most of the year, it looped lazily around its banks, shifting slightly with the ebb and rise of sandy water. But Dad had seen a three-and-a-half-foot wall of water (He said he could hear it, thundering dully in the distance, half an hour before it hit.) pushing tree trunks, planks, smashed boats ahead of it, inundating sandbars and salt cedars. Three and a half feet was an all-time record. But a flood, if it came fast or slow, could swell the river from a trickle you could throw a rock across to a giant a mile wide or more. Once he had swum it both ways when it was a mile and a half wide, bank to bank, just to show he could.

If I had thought Dad was exaggerating, I only had to walk through the woods, looking up in the trees. There, well above ground level, were mud-covered chicken coops, storage sheds, and refrigerator carcasses, frozen in clutching limbs. It must have been hard on a family, I pondered, to lose a crop when a flood like that swept over the bottoms.

But the opposite was just as likely, it being just as possible to lose a crop or a herd of cattle to a drought as to a flood. During the 1930s, the river dried up entirely, leaving only shallow pools of water separated by drifting sand. At night, a small trickle would flow, not an inch thick, between the pools. Red River water is brackish, thick with minerals, not good for cattle. But Grandpa brought his stock down off the prairies and managed to keep them alive on river water. When the grass was exhausted he bought an oxyacetylene torch and burnt off the spines of the prickly pear cactus, in the process cooking them. The cattle seemed to like prickly pear better than the grass.

The river's inconstancy can be summed up in the epic of cousin Rosa's oilwell. The Red River from the Texas bank all the way across to and including the real estate on its north side, belongs by law to Oklahoma. One day the river shifted, and Rosa's lone oil well turned up on the Oklahoma side, the property of the man who owned the land there. Legally nothing could be done. Four years later the river changed course again, and Rosa got her well back.

I have often said that Texas has no climate, only weather, and that the weather consists of long periods of boredom broken by violence. So with the river.

Besides the sprawl of river, and woods, and the ghosts of departed creatures, the stories focused on places.

Not far from our camp, the last spring that still flowed in that part of the river bottom trickled through a retinue of ferns. It had once been a deep blue hole of clear water, source of a small creek. If it was a small, nondescript place in the river bottom, that spring—which never had a name—was to have an unlikely intersection with history. One part of our family, the Ligons, had come to the river just before the Civil War from Clay County, Missouri, where they had been friends with the James family. The James, for all their reputation, were substantial people; Frank and Jesse's father was a Baptist preacher. That was how it happened that my great-grandmother, Rosa Ligon Gunter, had danced with Jesse James, at cotillions, before the Civil War. It also explained how it was that Frank and Jesse hid out on the Ligon place, camping by that spring, after the war. People said that the sheriff of Cooke County spent an inordinate amount of time in the south part of the county while the James brothers were encamped by the river, to the north. If Sivell's Bend was remote, however, news did travel. Finally, great-grandma had to go down to the spring and tell Frank and Jesse it was time for them to leave. "Yes ma'am," they said and began packing up. "Yes ma'am, we understand." They were gentlemen, Dad said. They were real gentlemen.

Half a mile from the spring stood a log cabin, less than six feet square and not more than five feet high. The roof was gone except for the ridge pole, and any chinking that had bound its logs was long vanished. It was, Dad said, a French trapper's cabin, the oldest structure in Cooke County, dating from the early 1830s. When the first settlers arrived they found it, next to a hillside seep spring that had now dried up. As a boy I tried to lie down in it, but could not stretch out full length. That trapper must have been a very small man, to have stayed there. He may have had several cabins, used as brief way stations on his trips up and down river.

Past the remains of the cabin sprawled a big slough, bordered by thickets of salt cedar and willow. Fifteen to twenty feet wide and around a hundred yards long, it filled in spring overflows and dried in the summer heat. In the dry times, fish struggled there to survive, lying flat in the shallows or, mouths out of the water, sucking hot summer air. One spring, people noticed not so much a huge fish as its wake, roiling the sandy water. As the water level fell, it was unmistakable: a massive fish patrolled the slough endlessly, restlessly, from one end to the other, making waves on the clay bank.

A local man, Mr. Treacher, studied the slough for several days, concluding triumphantly that a huge old catfish inhabited it. He then sent out an invitation up and down the river for a big fish fry. A week later the feast day arrived. Grandpa recalled that there were over a hundred people in wagons and Model T's waiting as Mr. Treacher pushed a skiff into the slough and stood triumphantly in the bow like Captain Ahab, a pitchfork raised triumphantly in his hands. Mr. Treacher shouted and drove the pitchfork straight down. There was a froth of bloody water, a piercing shout from Mr. Treacher (who, slapped hard by the pitchfork, fell in the water), and the thrashing of the fish, whose tail broke the skiff siding, and sent it to the bottom.

A huge old catfish though its meat might taste "gamey" or "muddy"—I have heard both terms used—will provide plenty of meat, even for a big crowd. Unfortunately the monster in the slough was not a catfish but an alligator gar: armor-plated, gristly, and inedible. Unless you want to eat gristle, and bone, and fatty meat you wouldn't eat alligator gar, not unless you were starving. When beached, the monster measured close to eight feet long—the biggest, bigger than anyone had ever seen. It would have weighed nearly three hundred pounds, if anybody had wanted to drag it to a scale and weigh it. Mr. Treacher left while men went out to the river to catch enough catfish to feed the onlookers.

Every time I passed that slough, I thought of Mr. Treacher. They say that he never came back to the river bottom after that. Not to that part of it, anyhow.

Mark Twain said that when he left home at the age of 20 his father was the most ignorant, backward man he ever knew, but when he returned at 21, it was amazing how much his old man had learned. What was true of his father was true of mine, but it took me a lot longer than a year to see it. The land was gone. Grandpa had sold the last of it shortly after I was born. The life it had supported was vanishing as old-timers died out and people moved to town. Paved roads and brush hogs cleared away timber and over-hunting cut down the game. Dad gave me the only thing he could: a heritage.

But heritages work in different ways in different people. The boy Dad had raised to be an athlete, an Aggie, and an engineer went off the tracks somewhere. On the Red River, he had seen a world cut down, diminished, taken away. Now he saw in a different place the same parallel: this time with bulldozers, and power saws, and thousand-acre clear cuts. Dad never could understand why I put so much into trying to save the Big Thicket. Maybe he was too close to see it. I was, too.

So I was prepared, by a kind of convergent evolution, to understand Lance Rosier well before we actually met, even before I chanced to pick up a flashy silver and magenta Texas book at the college bookstore. We were alike. And yet we were different. Different enough that much about Lance continued to puzzle me.

It wasn't his Frenchness that turned him into a conservationist: but it is hard to say what did. French ancestry could be swept under the rug. (The Rosier children finally shamed their father into not speaking French.) Nor was it the culture of Southeast Texas that made the difference. True, Saratoga, his home, was in the middle of the shaggy Big Thicket wilderness. But few if any of those who lived there were like Lance Rosier. The preferred activities for young men there were, and still are, hunting and football. The economy of the place was based on timbering and the nearby oil fields. Lance drifted, out in the woods, learning the name of birds, trees, flowers, and frogs. That was no small task in an area as biologically diverse as any in North America. He began to buy nature books and encyclopedias. "Why he don't do nothin' but prowl them woods," people would mutter. Damn strange guy.

For all his love and knowledge of nature, he was not initially a conservationist. For several years, he made a living as a surveyor's guide and as a "spotter": someone who finds stands of saleable timber for sawmill operators. But as the destruction by lumber operators became more and more apparent, he became increasingly determined to defend what was left. The turning point was probably the Big Thicket Biological Survey of 1936–37. Scientists who converged on the region from major Texas universities found themselves dependent on this slight, reticent man for the locations of plant communities, heron rookeries, tree-dwelling orchids. To get to know an area in which dry western, wet eastern, temperate northern and subtropical Gulf plant species mix incongruously was not easy. It took someone like Lance, a student of both local nuance and scientific abstraction, to be an effective guide there.

When the scientists had gone, Lance continued his work, becoming a kind of pied piper for all those curious about the Thicket: birdwatchers, amateur botanists, conservationists, biologists looking for specimens, ladies' clubs on backwoods forays, odd characters like myself who appeared without warning on his doorstep. Without fail he accompanied us all, exploring the palmetto jungles on Pine Island Bayou or the cypress-tupelo swamps along Village Creek, leading us to groves of giant magnolias, longleaf pine savannahs, insect-eating plant bogs. He cast a spell of total familiarity, kneeling to cup a wildflower in his hand, pointing out the now huge oak his grandfather had planted when the family first settled near Saratoga, talking to a golden spider as it wandered peacefully across his forearm and onto an adjacent branch.

The results of his quiet teaching were important, even vital. Nearly every leader in the struggle (beginning in 1964) to create a nature preserve in the Big Thicket was baptized by Lance: every leader, and most of the troops, in the nucleus of the early Big Thicket Association. He did not live to see the victory. Lance died in 1970, frustrated by the pile-up of Big Thicket bills in Congress and by unending friction in the Texas congressional delegation.

But to the end he insisted that the politicians would eventually have to act. He was right. In October 1974, an 84,500-acre Big Thicket National Biological Preserve was signed into law by President Gerald Ford. Lance would have been truly pleased. Not only did the preserve contain samples of virtually every major habitat in the region, including long stretches of the Neches River and Pine Island Bayou; it was also the first biological preserve in the history of the National Park Service, a nature sanctuary devoted not to scenery, but to ecology *per se*. And one of its units—the largest, in fact, at 24,942 acres—was named after Lance Rosier. It isn't often that one gets to see such a pure case of poetic justice. Once considered the black sheep of his family, now it is through him that the family name lives on.

If Lance would have been pleased with the preserve, he would have been still more pleased with what has happened since its creation: the addition of a 40-mile corridor down Big Sandy-Village Creek and a "canyonlands" unit on the Neches River (these later still in contention but liable to happen). These and other additions make Southeast Texas a kind of widely-spaced conservationist checkerboard. It is imperfect to be sure, not so much planned as somehow just happening. But it is infinitely superior to the total destruction—wall-to-wall clearcutting—that *would have* occurred. The Lance Rosier Unit of the Big Thicket National Preserve is both a real and a mythical place, real because it is a definite piece of real estate, mythical because, at least for many of us, the spirit of its patient, stubborn namesake continues to preside over its looping cypress-studded bayous, isolated ponds, and pine uplands. But you don't have to take my word for it. The Rosier Unit is open to anyone, day or night. Some early morning take the sandy road off the highway just east of Saratoga and head south. A hawk will be soaring above the treetops. A fox or an armadillo will scurry across the road and vanish. The road dust will tell tales of snakes, bobcats, wild hogs: exploring, encountering each other, departing into the undergrowth. With a little effort you can find it, down the road, the oak tree Lance's grandfather planted all those years ago, before the Civil War. It is massive, many-branched, and soaring, draped with Spanish moss and resurrection fern.

In February 1970, Roy and Karen Hamric, and Elizabeth, my wife, and I, visited Lance at Saratoga. He had fallen and broken his hip, but the doctors urged him to get out and walk. He levered himself up with a cane, stepped painfully off the front porch, and asked us to go out to the Bayou.

There was something about Lance that day that troubled us, besides his hip. He seemed wizened, withdrawn, tired. His passion for nature was as real as ever. But he was forcing himself, almost, giving a well-learned speech.

A week before Lance died, Roy Hamric visited him at a hospital in Beaumont.

Lance talked about the Thicket—about how it had been cut back through the years and how clearcutting was destroying the hardwoods. He talked about whether there still could be ivory-billed woodpeckers and about how orchids were coming back around the Hyatt bogs and pinelands. There was a big water oak outside the window. As they talked, hundreds, then thousands of monarch butterflies began landing there, carpeting the oak with a living mosaic of orange and black. Lance said he was tired now and needed to sleep. He wanted Roy to come back when he had got back his strength. Roy agreed. They stared at the mass of butterflies.

"Aren't they beautiful," Lance said.

"Aren't they beautiful."

That was decades ago now, longer than I like to think. I would rather eclipse all that time and think of Lance as alive now. Alive and hiking, discoursing to the herons and the ferns. But though that cannot be, the loss of Lance and the passage of time provide one real consolation. They have taught me the very special debt that I owe him. Without intending to, without realizing it, Lance taught me who I really was: who I had already been without recognizing it. What I had learned in the prairies, brushwood, and limestone country of the Red River came through Lance in me into a new focus, framing a green, tangled subtropical land in a way I could not have imagined on my own. That in turn changed how I could see not only the Red River but all rivers—all prairies, woods, swamps, bayous. It changed everything.

Prairie, David Taylor

CHAPTER 5

BARBARA "BARNEY" NELSON

THAT ONE-EYED HEREFORD MULEY

Barbara "Barney" Nelson has published six books, the most recent is *God's Country or Devil's Playground: The Best Nature Writing from the Big Bend of Texas*. In addition, her scholarly essays appear in three recent collections about Henry David Thoreau, Mary Austin, and Edward Abbey. She has also published numerous popular press essays, photographs, and poetry—the most recent is "My First Daughter was an Antelope" in *Heart Shots: Women Write About Hunting* (edited by Mary Stange, Stackpole, 2003). Nelson is an associate professor of English at Sul Ross State University in Alpine. Nelson's work mixes the rural, agricultural voice with nature writing.

> *"I am interested in exploring*
> *my personal ecology.*
> *I live from deer;*
> *this voice*
> *has been fed from deer.*
> *I appreciate the fact that I am made*
> *out of the animal*
> *I love."*
>
> — *Richard Nelson*

I was sitting in a boring literature class one day, a shiny-faced, idealistic undergraduate, thinking about boys—only I had started calling them men. I was an Animal Science major, studying to become a ranch manager, or a cowboy's wife, whichever came first.

My college sat on the side of a mountain, as most colleges do so that college professors can look down upon the town from a lofty perch. So, I was watching buzzards out the classroom window, almost at eye level. The professor was asking us to decide whether Edward Abbey's narrative voice should be classified as homodiegetic or autodiegetic—yawn.

The buzzards were putting me to sleep. Buzzards drift so aimlessly and effortlessly on thermals, especially in the hot rimrocked desert country of West Texas. But just as my eyelids were drooping, the big black birds seemed suddenly to change gears.

Instead of drifting, they began to circle with more of a purpose. Is a cow dead down there on main street? I wondered if they had put to sleep the old cowboy, Nicasio Ramirez, who always sat on the corner in the sun. As the circle tightened, more and more buzzards appeared out of nowhere. First ten, then twenty, then I was watching 100, then 1000 buzzards circle right outside my classroom window. It was a once in a lifetime sight!

I raised my hand.

"Sir!" I stammered excitedly, "The buzzards are gathering to fly south right outside the window! There are thousands of them!"

The professor frowned, told me to keep my mind in class and went on about Abbey. I changed my major to English that day. The professor probably thought his lecture had inspired me, and it did. I decided right there in that classroom, as the buzzards broke their circle and headed south, that *I* should be teaching Abbey.

One of my favorite images, which appears over and over in Ed Abbey's books, is a cowboy, riding along, spending his life and imagination looking at a shit-encrusted, fly-clouded, jouncing cow's butt. Chuckle.

Western movies have always left the cowshit and horseshit out, ever notice that? Shit just doesn't fit into the Western myth. Buffalo chips might be useful as fuel, but not cow chips—well, maybe in India, but not in the American West.

Anyone who doesn't believe in cowshit would not want to brand Brammer calves—ever—even with the toe of their boot over the spout. They wouldn't want to be hit by a cow tail when the yuccas are blooming, wouldn't want to shove an arm up a heifer's cervix to pull a calf, wouldn't want to climb into crowding chutes when spring grass is green, wouldn't like "mud" without rain, scours, flat rocks, scared wild cows—yup, real cows do shit, and I've spent a lot of years staring at their Southern ends. My imagination is probably ruined.

As a matter of fact, one of my fondest memories and best stories involves a hot, sleepy afternoon moving bulls, the world's slowest, most boring job. Bobbing in my saddle after a big dinner, I suddenly woke up to realize that the biggest bull had switched his tail over one of my bridle reins and was now clamped down hard. My horse, of course, wanted air—now. Luckily, being in Texas, I was using split leather reins instead of a looped McCarty or rawhide reins and *romal*, so I quickly dropped the captured rein and let the wreck work itself out. When everything finally came loose and stopped, I was still horseback, no bones broken, and my bridle still in one piece. My rein had simply slid through between the bull's tightly clamped tail and his butt. The green sticky rein I rode with the rest of the day imprinted the cheap lesson forever on my memory.

Cowshit creates memories. When it appears between your sandaled toes, under hatbrims, inside a torn shirt pocket, up a pantleg, gets into boots or eyes or hair, is imbedded between your teeth, smeared all over your rope—usually you have just finished learning a cheap lesson. The cowshit sort of says, "And don't ever try that again."

I had a neighbor once who lived about ten miles down the dirt road toward town. Our underground water had been polluted by oil fields (which was enabling the ranchers who owned the places where we worked to stay in the cow business). I caught drinking water off my tin roof and stored it in a cistern. My neighbor, however, was horrified that I would drink birdshit. Her water came from a brown muddy cow tank which turned green in the summer. Nobody ever got sick drinking after cows, she said, but birds she didn't quite trust.

I agreed. After a morning of flanking calves and gripping slimy tails, I seldom bothered to wash my hands before dinner. My healthy little daughter grew up having shit fights (starting out dry, ending wet) with her wild little country kid friends and none of them ever missed a day of school because of illness. Playing hooky maybe, but sick—never.

But my camp was on a hill, no muddy cowtank close by. And cows attract a lot of birds. There was never a time during summer when at least a half-dozen vermilion flycatchers weren't diving around my yard. My trees bloomed with scarlet tanagers, summer tanagers, and orioles. Herds of deafening scissortails woke me up every morning long before daylight. So, I had to drink birdshit. As Wally McRae says, cowshit is just grass and water, but flies and water? Yuck.

So, if I love cows this much, how can I read Abbey's condemning essay "Free Speech: The Cowboy and His Cow" and still love Abbey? He was a sexist, a drunk, an opinionated old fart—just like most of my closest friends. It is comforting to know how someone thinks.

When Abbey says ranches today are tax write-offs for corporations, investment syndicates, land and cattle companies (heavy on the land), and that "Western cattlemen are nothing more than welfare parasites"—I don't even wince. He's not talking about me. He makes a careful distinction between wage-earning cowboys and wannabes, between ranchers and instant rednecks, nouveau Westerners and old weather-beaten Westerners, between pet horses and working horses, between cow ranching and elk or dude ranching, between inheritors and heritage, between the mythic American horseback knight (white hat) and the dumb cowboy who stares at a cow's butt all day (black hat).

Over-grazing. Yeah, I winced at that, maybe even bled. Even though I don't feel too patronizingly protective toward plants—I've seen what they can do to mountains, cement, and asphalt—I still can't put over-grazing in the same humorous category as cowshit. So, for the past ten years, ever since a cowboy friend mailed me a dog-eared copy of Abbey's damn essay, I have been studying everything I can find about grass and grazing and historical land uses and predator/prey relationships and fire and Allan Savory and water tables and pampas grass and diversity and mass extinctions and mourning dove habitat and plate tectonics and soil composition and weather patterns and on and on and on and on.

When Abbey said domestic animals, like humans, will improve if hunted, was he talking to me?

Abbey writes about a mountain lion following him through Arizona's Arrivipa Canyon—a huge pile of slick rock. But, years before Abbey ever saw that canyon, while wolves still roamed it, I gathered cattle and branded calves there. One mis-step and a shod horse's hoof would slide straight down those slick rocks for a half-mile. Carefully worn pale trails that followed the levelest footing across the backbone of that sheer rock country were terrifyingly faint. The only way to gather it was to climb to that backbone and ride each rib. Someone either braver or dumber than I made those trails.

Finding a trail means that someone has already passed here safely, and sometimes that is important. I have traveled Abbey's road and sometimes he has traveled mine. I fell in love two different summers while working at the Grand Canyon. I've been into the abyss. I've rafted the Rio Grande and ridden the Chisos trails. I've run my own cattle at the foot of the Guadalupes and in the desert beyond Boquillas Canyon. I've seen the far side of Mexico's mountains and glimpsed its wild cattle through the brush. I've pulled up my share of survey stakes and slept with the GRIZ. I've drunk from some of the most remote and well-hidden water holes in the West. My dad, like Abbey's, was a pot-hunter, not a sportsman. My dad and brother twice won second place in the same varmint calling contest Abbey cusses at the end of *One Life at a Time, Please*. But I'm not ashamed.

On the Chihuahuan desert where I have lived for the past 30 years, grass is short, bunched, and dust colored. Passers-through sometimes can't see it. Visibility improves at sundown when the late evening light bathes the land in fuzzy gold. Except for the grass, this desert is like all deserts: hot, dry, and mute. Here green is not garish like '50s neon, but greyed, faded, and brittle. In the best of years native gramas stay green only about two weeks. People who love this country prefer their grasses in khaki. Blue is not royal but sun bleached like faded denim. No lipstick company would copy desert reds unless their customers wanted dignity instead of attention. Desert colors are not aggressive. They don't compete, don't shout. They steal your heart with a whisper.

The ground is rocky, rainfall sporadic, water sources tiny—the grass desert's three greatest assets. If any one of these factors were changed, this country would fill with something else: farms, industry, cities, golf courses. Wide 50-mile flats are broken by mountains but not mountain ranges. Even mountains in this country prefer to live scattered. Sometimes one, sometimes two, no more than four or five are bunched together. A local lion trapper calls them "mountain islands." He says they keep our lion population viable by causing sometimes 500-mile migrations for dispersing kittens.

Some call our mountains ghost mountains and say at night they go away to play with other mountains, but I can see the mountains even at night. We also call the lions our ghost cat. Except for trappers and hunters, one must believe in mountain lions rather than see them. I believe. Trapper friends have shown me their tracks, their scat, their scrapings. A pretty good tracker myself, I can't find their sign or read it without help from a lion hunter. I once found a dead deer covered with lion trash, less than a mile from town. Once, I think I heard one growl at my dog. In Northern California, in that half-light of gray dawn, maybe I saw one trotting easily with a little band of deer. When my presence became known, one of the gray animals, who seemed to be trailing a long tail, streaked away from the deer herd. It stopped just at the break of a hill to look at me when I whistled—typical coyote behavior, but normally not lion behavior. As Hawthorne would say, my eyes could have been playing tricks in the half-light. Maybe I imagined the tail. Maybe some lions stop for a whistle like coyotes.

Mountain lions are very territorial. Where mountains appear in belts of wide, timbered ranges, lion territories are small, maybe only five square miles. Lions don't seem to like flat land, so a mountain island sometimes becomes home to only one lion, and by claiming the mountain, he or she may claim 200 square miles or more. Passers-through, smelling the territory markers, keep loping, unless the smell tells them that the occupant is weak or old or in heat. Studies done in Big Bend National Park show that one lion will claim the same territory sometimes for generations, sometimes until the patriarch or matriarch becomes sterile. More happily, before the race dies out, an aggressive kitten or a hunter will kill and replace an aging mother or an aging male. But time, heat, and distance frustrate the efforts of lion hunters. A few minutes after sunrise, scent trails evaporate. Ghosts.

When survival depends upon limited food supplies, mothers kill kittens, females kill males, and kittens who want to survive hit the trail. Prey bases are precious. Dispersing kittens and ragged grandparents sometimes end up in town, living for a while on pets, until the local news-paper editor looks up from morning coffee and spots tawny fur in the apple tree. I find few mountain lion stories in Native American collec-tions, but in the grass desert, everyone has a lion story. One enterprising young lion followed a dog through a pet-door entrance at the back of a local restaurant, killed the dog in the kitchen, drug it back out the pet door and into the rocks to eat and cover with litter for later.

But few lions end up on the flats except when passing through. Local ranchers have capitalized on this knowledge by raising colts—a lion delicacy—in the flats. One border rancher who likes to test bound-aries is raising a small band of sheep on his flats—just to prove he can attract eagles back into this country and defy environmentalists. He blames lack of eagles on protection. He says the sky here used to be full of eagles until local sheepmen were put out of business. With no prey base, the eagles disappeared. So, he wants to feed eagles again and somehow he thinks that will make "those damn environmentalists" mad.

For 13 years I lived on a big ghost mountain ranch whose scent markers enclosed over 220 square miles, most of it fenced only by rimrock and canyon. When gathering cattle in this country, we would find the same cow in the same place, year after year. The ranch raised horned Herefords, and although they never drew blood, they hooked and horned each other unmercifully until some kind of status quo was reached, even inside corrals. Cows in my country become very territorial. Ideal country to a cow is flat. Although cows seldom kill one another, they are cruel when defending their territories. Old cows, young cows, lame cows, cows with any kind of weakness, even if just lack of courage, are pushed to the fringes. Like wolves, the alpha males and females eat first and best. But, like wolves, they also babysit each other's kids. Like wolves, cows are very careful where they step. Rocks make their feet sore. One can follow their meandering soft dusty water trails for miles and never find a pebble. Wolves loved to trot down those soft trails too—one of their downfalls.

The cows who hold the territory along streams which run through the flats are the most aggressive, but I always liked best the ones who ranged up on the rocky points with the lions. Seems like they always had the best calves and the longest horns, but maybe I just wanted that to be true because my territories too were always easy to defend because no one else wanted them. I like horned cattle. I believe that if you take away their horns, like women, they become stupid and helpless. They can't defend their territories, they can't protect their calves.

But, then, I also remember an old one-eyed Hereford muley who didn't fit the stereotypes. In her honor, I would like to speak a word for absolute freedom and wildness.

A partner and I once bought some old cows that local ranchers were selling. When a rancher sells an old cow, he thinks she won't make another winter and he wants to sell her before she crumbles. We thought we might be able to buy these old cows cheap, squeeze one more calf out of them, and get ourselves a start in the cow business.

We also leased country the ranchers didn't want. It was too rough, too remote, too prone to losing its water sources in dry years. The country was called "Dry Canyon." Ranchers sometimes discover a piece of country within their territories where water dries up too often, where cow teeth wear out too fast, or where calf numbers are low because bulls can't handle the steep terrain well enough to get around and breed the cows. Sometimes when country never makes a profit and some honest, hard-working young kids come along who want to try to put together something of their own, a benevolent rancher might lease that bad country. Bankers will also sometimes loan money to young, hard-working, proud people who will somehow pay back their debts. And, as the old ranchers, the banker, and the young kids know—gambling sometimes works.

So, we leased Dry Canyon, put down our scent markers, and we had a plan. Young healthy heifers were too expensive and Dry Canyon too remote to husband them through their first calf. Prime cows were impossible to buy at any price, so we carefully selected and bought the 20 best grannies we could find. We had also leased some state park land which would make a good holding pasture and had enough grazing for about a month. The grannies could recover their strength there after their calves were shipped. The park needed the grass mowed a little to keep the fire hazard down. We could hold our grannies on that country and wait for good cool fall weather to trail them into Dry Canyon. Dependable cool weather in the desert doesn't come sometimes until December.

Dry Canyon was in great shape to receive them. Grass was good and every pocket had caught a little water. We planned to drop the grannies on the rim which looked off into Big Aguja Canyon and gradually move them, as water sources dried up on the rim, down toward the most dependable water in the bottom of Dry Canyon, saving that grass until last.

We knew the drive in would be hard on them, up and down steep mountain trails, no water until the end. But once we got them to the lease, all the drives from then on would be mostly down hill as they got heavier and heavier with calf. They wouldn't have to—and we knew they couldn't, no matter what—climb back out until they were much thinner, with their calves walking on their own feet. It wouldn't be easy for the old ladies.

But, it was a good gamble.

We had the grannies preg-checked by a vet to insure a spring calf. We wouldn't need a bull. If the venture worked, we'd have the old cows to sell at a better price, hopefully, than we gave for them, and a calf too. We'd pay back the bank, borrow less money next time, and make another gamble until we could get a start. My partner and I were a little younger than the ranchers who were selling the old cows. We figured we could make longer circles horseback and we still believed in our own immortality.

All the cows were good native horned Herefords, except one. She came from a ranch we neighbored and seemed in good shape except for being hornless and one-eyed. She had evidently had cancer eye and an eye operation—which consisted of digging out the bad eye with a pocket knife and sewing the bloody hole shut. Bad eyes are a common problem in white-faced Herefords, especially those who live in desert country where sunlight is intense. Because she had a defect, and no horns, the horned cattle hooked her constantly.

The trail to Dry Canyon is only one cow wide. Steep rock walls rise and fall on each side, making cowboying difficult. We couldn't afford help. Even friends expect day-wages and a meal, and this was horse killing country. Four of us took on the job. My daughter's grandpa, over 70 years old, rode point to keep them on the trail. We didn't figure he would need to stop any runaways. The most patient rider, my little daughter, rode drag. We knew she would lolly gag along, happily sucking on her saddle strings, looking for birds and letting the cattle string out long and slow. Some people like a wide herd, but cows don't get as hot or as tired when allowed to trail one another in single file. The other two riders, myself and my partner, would ride swing, climbing up and down the cliffs at the sides of the herd, trying to keep the cattle strung out and trailing. But we soon discovered that two riders could ride along in front and chat, and two could ride along in the rear and chat. The old one-eyed cow, because the others picked on her, struck the lead and never stopped. The others simply followed, trying to hook her in the butt.

The one-eyed cow's habits became more interesting as the winter wore on. When we gathered the grannies to move them to the next water hole, the old one-eyed cow was already there. She had new salt and water trails well marked for the followers. As the herd moved in, she moved out, and sometimes one or two went with her.

Toward spring, we started finding dead cows and dogie calves. Although the grass held, the old cows were struggling too hard in the rough country, and the water was drying up fast. We found one cow down, still alive, but covered with black lice. Her calf, still nursing, had a ring of black lice around his white nose. I thought about Barry Lopez's theory about the "conversation of death." I wondered if the old cow had sacrificed herself to the lice for the sake of the herd, since none of the others were infested. Mother Nature has no sympathy for the weak. Someone called me Mother Nature once when I said anybody dumb enough to break a leg ought to be left there to die of thirst. We picked up the calf and shot the cow.

On the morning of the last move to more water, we rose in the dark and trailered our horses to the end of the road. The sky was turning gray as we stepped into the saddle and the March wind had already started to pick up. When I headed into Dry Canyon I always tried to be as prepared as I could for emergencies. I knew we would be without food, water, or help for many hours. Most cowboys I have known never carry food or canteens. They never carry first-aid kits. Not because of any fool-hardy attempt at heroics, but because if the day is going to be long enough to need food and water, then the horse doesn't need to be carrying one more ounce of weight. If the animal who is doing all the work can't drink or eat, reasons the cowboy, then the human the animal is packing around sure doesn't need anything. Horses should always eat and drink first.

Also, nobody happens down the trail in Dry Canyon. No photographers, no artists, no backpackers, no rangers, nobody. In my pocket was a tiny jar of Carmex, relief against the painful, bleeding chapped lips I knew would come after 18 hours in the saddle on a hot, windwhipped March day. Real cowboys grow moustaches to protect themselves from chapped lips. I can't seem to grow one.

Around my neck I had tied a cotton bandana which sorta matched my shirt. I hoped my partner would think it was just a dumb female fashion statement. I am cowboy enough to disdain the cotton bandana under normal conditions. In winter and fall, my neck rag is silk, like it ought to be. But I knew I would need no warmth today. River rafting had taught me the cooling effects of a cotton bandana soaked in water and tied around my neck, dripping. I thought that trick had saved my life at least twice. Dry Canyon had also taught me that bones break, oak brush limbs and yucca puncture, horse shoes come off, and bandages are hard to come by. So, I thought the bandana would be an inconspicuous first-aid kit for both myself and my horse.

Perhaps my immortality had already begun to crack.

The rest of my safety precautions were common cowboy gear. I wore high-heeled boots so my foot wouldn't slip through the stirrup in case my horse fell. I wore leather leggins to turn the brush from my largest veins and arteries. I wore a long-sleeved shirt and a broad-brimmed Navajo creased hat to turn the sun. I looked at the starry, cloudless sky and chose not to pack my slicker, which would just tear up anyway in Dry Canyon's brush. I wore tight-fitting cotton jeans that would not bunch up in wrinkles to rub the insides of my knees raw, and I wore no belt to catch on the saddle horn and tie me to a horse I might want to get away from. You can sometimes tell what kind of horses people ride by whether or not they wear belts.

And I was riding a new horse. As we mounted and started up the steep jeep trail that led into Dry Canyon, the wind tore at my hat. I tightened the stampede string which keeps it in place to act like a helmet to protect my feeble brain in case a limb or a rock tries to get me. But the wind was strong and getting stronger. I knew it would be an all-day battle to keep the hat in place and I knew I might need both hands to keep my horse under—not control, but maybe distraction. So I rode back to the truck, threw my hat in the cab and tied the cotton bandana around my hair to keep it out of my face. My head was now exposed to more danger than I usually risk, but I figured I would just lose my hat anyway as it sailed off into one of the deep canyons. If I got in a storm with my new horse, a real likely time would be when I grabbed too fast for a wind-loosened hat and was off-balance and one-handed.

My partner wears a hat with a much smaller brim, tightly curled on the sides, and has very little hair to keep it pulled down over. He never leaves his hat behind but he did lose it once, sunburned terribly, and I found it a couple of weeks later by following what I thought would be the wind's trail. I was right and the hat lay right where I expected it to be: due east, at the foot of the first dry creek bank where it could hide from the wind. That also happened one March.

Riding a new horse is like no other experience. My skin tingled with awareness. My eyes and ears and all six senses searched ahead for trouble while I pretended to be lost in thought and relaxed. I knew the wind would pick up my long-fringed leather leggins and throw them at my horse's neck. So, nonchalantly, I fiddled with them and flipped them around, first one and then the other, getting my horse used to the booger, as I chatted with my partner. Up ahead, somewhere in the darkness, I heard the wind hit the dry leaves of a live oak and shake it like an Indian rattle. Live oaks do their fall shedding in the spring for some reason. Had we been beside the tree at that moment, I'd have jumped with fright and startled my horse. Charlie Siringo used to claim that cowboys rode horses so much they, too, would shy at a wind-blown piece of paper when they walked down a sidewalk in town. I always believed it was the other way around, that cowboys taught horses to shy at paper.

It's like riding over a covey of quail and have them hit the air under you, or jumping a big jackrabbit out of its shade. The horse sees those sights in its home pasture daily, but becomes frightened because the rider tenses for action and the horse doesn't see the danger which his rider has evidently seen. There was a bright purple prickly pear patch in the East Pruitt pasture that every horse in my string shied at. Those same purple cactus were everywhere, so it must have started when I became startled in that spot for some reason. The next time we passed it, the horse remembered and became tense. Then, expecting the horse to get tense, I'd tense in that spot. Then, forgetting which horse got nervous there, I'd tense up no matter which one I was riding, and so it went until every horse I rode knew that particular purple cactus patch. Anyway, I mentally prepared myself to remain calm when the wind rattled a live oak beside me today. There were no live oaks in this horse's home pasture.

The blowing dust and tiny rocks were already getting into my hair, eyes, and nose. This would be a black booger day. I cleared my throat repeatedly, puffed my cheeks full of air and shook my head violently, expelling wind to drive out the dust like an escaped balloon—pretending to cuss the weather. If I had had any money in my pocket, I'd have been jingling that too. I kept at this coughing, cursing, leggin-flipping frenzy until the wind finally hit a tree next to me and my horse didn't bat an eye.

After the first long uphill pull, my horse's head began to swing easily between the slack reins of my McCarty and neither wind nor snapping leather fringe seemed to worry him enough to expend more energy than necessary. Perhaps because of the weather, the climb, and the early hour, the horse knew this was going to be a long, long day and he better save his energy. So, he finally convinced me to relax and save mine too.

Many hours later, when we got our wobbling old grannies to the expected water hole, it was dry. We pushed on to the next—also dry. We were in trouble. Could the old cows live to reach the last water hole on the rim of the canyon, and if they lived to reach it, would there be water? Would any of them still be alive the next time we came back? This was too much stress on old cattle. The gambling odds had suddenly shifted. Stumbling, staggering, stringing saliva with every agonized step, the old ladies inched their way toward the last water hole. I cussed, jerked on the reins and drove spurs into my horse unmercifully. He traveled too fast. He pushed too hard. I had to keep circling him to keep him backed off the old cows. The more I tried to slow him down, the more antsy he became. I cussed. I jerked him around. I don't think I ever treated a horse worse.

My own frustration, knowing we had lost the gamble, was coming out in the horse. His neck and shoulders were covered with white lather. I think I wanted him to buck me off, hurt me, give me a reason to quit.

We didn't make it. That day, when we reached the last water hole, the old cows just stood and drooled. The country rose in a circle almost straight up from the water hole—yearling country. We looked around and knew we'd find most of these old cows lying right where they stood the next time we rode in. But, as we sat there, letting our horses drink and avoiding each other's eyes, I noticed the old one-eyed cow slip off over the rim and down a deer trail. She was pushing on to the more permanent water and grass in the canyon below. I marked the spot in my memory. We might need that trail.

Back in civilization, another six hours later, we were told winds had been clocked at over 100 miles per hour in the mountains that day. A roof had blown off at the airport and trees had blown down on the college campus. I had forgotten all about the wind.

By spring only ten cows and fifteen calves remained alive, but one of them was the one-eyed muley. She had raised a good calf and she led us back out. I made up my mind that when shipping time came, I'd insist on running her one more year.

But I didn't. We cut our losses and finally, years later, repaid the debt. We gave up the Dry Canyon lease and never went back. But maybe we should have. That country made good horses. It raised my daughter horseback. It taught me to look at a one-eyed cow with respect, something my more expensive college education never did.

But I wouldn't call the old one-eyed cow wild, exactly. I've known some cows who were so wild they couldn't be gathered. Constantly pursued by some of the West's finest cowboys, those phantom cows lived long, wild lives, were never branded, and learned not to leave tracks. (My lion runnin' friend, Roy McBride, always interrupts my story here to correct me and say that they did leave tracks. But I remind Roy that only he could see them. For the rest of us there were no tracks.) I've seen mule deer in Texas who were shot at every deer season, and often by poachers between, who did not run from an approaching pickup, horse, or foot traveler. But nobody in a pickup and few people horseback ever catch a glimpse of renegade cattle. Foot travelers better hope they don't.

I have worked cattle in places where, when I heard a twig snap, I had a few tense moments in which to decide whether to run for my life or give chase. Some of those old wild, sharp-horned, brush-popper cows came out of a manzanita thicket like a freight train, aiming for my horse's belly. I've helped pull weak cows out of deep mud where they had bogged down, only to have them turn and try to kill me for my efforts. Thoreau in his sissy-sounding nineteenth century words called it "sportiveness in cattle" and said it was usually "unexpected." They'll nearly all try to kill you though, so you start expecting it; then you are disappointed if they don't.

Cows are often called stupid when they step on a cowboy's foot, when they take his horse away from him, when they blow snot down his neck while he's trying to brand their calf. They are called stupid when they get old, smooth-mouthed, stiff-jointed, and refuse to get on the truck that will permanently take them away from their pastures. They are called stupid when they silently lose a tracker in noisy, slippery shale, or lie down and disappear behind a foot-high bush. They are called stupid when they out-hear, out-see, and out-smell their tracker. I've heard college-educated cowboys humbly admit they had been outsmarted by a stupid cow.

Although ranchers "protect" cows in order to raise every calf, the cow is quite capable of taking care of herself. Even in the heyday of the wolf, dinners of baby calf were few. According to my friend Roy, the wolf had much better success with weaned yearlings. Antelope and deer often bed down with horned mama cows while fawns are young. I know one Montana rancher who has so much faith in his own ornery cows that he voluntarily makes a home for Yellowstone's problem grizzly bears who can't get along with tourists. "I seldom have trouble with trespassers," he says with a sly grin.

Maybe the number of times an animal has killed a man should determine wildness? The cow beats the griz a hundred times over. I once knew a crippled cow, down and paralyzed from calving, who still almost killed a cowboy. As he tried to help her drink from a bucket, she hooked him down, pounded, slashed, and scraped him through the brush and rocks for several long minutes before he was finally able to crawl for his life. As Thoreau would say, she was "not yet subdued to man."

I've helped pull calves from wild heifers, down and dying trying to deliver a backwards calf, who would jump up and run off and leave their calves unlicked because they smelled like a human. Like all wild animals, cows react to changes in weather, showing restlessness and nervousness when a storm is brewing. I've seen 300 heifers sniff the breeze off a Blue Norther, throw number nines in their tails and stampede. Or, as Thoreau would say, they were "running about and frisking in unwieldy sport" as they "shook their heads, raised their tails and rushed up and down a hill."

Thoreau enjoyed seeing his neighbor's cow break out of her pasture early in the spring and boldly swim the river like the buffalo. I've seen cattle hump up with their snow-covered backs against the wind, like buffalo, and wait patiently for the three-day thaw they seemed to know was coming. I've seen them break ice for a drink. Bison will sweep snow away with their heads in order to find feed, but cows prefer to let the wind do the work and will drift until they find a wind-swept mesa. History is full of tales of abandoned cow herds left to die in a blizzard and found alive with new calves the following spring. Of course those stories happened in the days before fences stopped cows from drifting. And sometimes the snow comes just too deep and neither cows, nor bison, nor caribou make it.

Like all animals, cows have to be taught to eat hay or feed cubes. This doesn't come naturally. On some big desert ranches where cows are never taught, a drouth can wipe out an entire herd. I've seen antelope learn to come to the feedground to eat. Friends, Bill and Sherry Dugan, used to feed hay to the Yellowstone elk every winter using sleighs and their big work horses, yet I've known wild cows who starved themselves to death once corralled.

In Arizona, near Mayer, the winter of 1966 or '67, I helped drag hay, one bale at a time behind a snowmobile, to little bands of cows found trapped under pine trees where they had tramped out their own deep snow prison. They were so hungry and desperate, they were eating each other's tails, yet some wouldn't eat the hay I brought to them. In normal weather, these were the wild cows that no one ever saw. That winter many Navajos also starved, and antelope stood next to helicopter-dropped hay and refused to eat. Lulled into carelessness mild winter after mild winter, Arizonans were unprepared. I would bet Arizonans are unprepared today.

In spite of their wildness, classic cow characters to compare with Hemingway's marlin, Faulkner's bear, or London's dog/wolves are non-existent, even in cowboy literature. This surprises me because everyone I know has a story about some bull, some cow, some heifer, some steer or some calf. A few characters show up in cowboy poetry: Bruce Kiskaddon's "Long Eared Bull," "The Cow and Calf," "A Calf's Troubles," and Gail Gardner's "The Sierry Petes" which casts the devil as a maverick steer.

In cowboy fiction I can think of only one good cow character: J. P. S. Brown's old maverick steer, Sun Spot. Brown characterizes the steer in such a way that I know the steer—how he likes to nap on south-facing slopes to warm the white spot on his side, how he has managed to evade capture, where he drinks, where he eats. The cowboys, of course, catch him, and of course, turn him loose.

The only thing I don't like about Brown's portrait is the name. I've never named a cow. Cows are not pets. The "too familiar" relationship between person and pet seems like a disrespectful relationship somehow. I'm sure it could be interpreted as distancing yourself from what you will eat, but milkpen calves and the steers who get kept up and put on feed for slaughter usually do get named and petted. Naming an old range cow just seems like something the cow wouldn't like. I got to know a lot of them quite well, but I always called them respectfully "that old high-horned cow who hangs out at Last Chance" or "that old one-eyed Hereford muley."

Clear Creek, David Taylor

CHAPTER 6

JOE NICK PATOSKI

SPRINGS

Joe Nick Patoski lives, works, plays, and swims near the Hill Country village of Wimberley. He's been writing about Texas and Texans for more than 35 years.

Of all the features that define the natural state of Texas, nothing speaks to me like springs do. As the source of water in its purest, most pristine form, springs are the basic building block of life. They present themselves in a manner as miraculous as birth itself, gestating in the womblike darkness of an aquifer deep underground until pressure percolates, pushes, and forces it up through cracks, fissures, and faults in the limestone cap until it bubbles, seeps, sometimes even gushes to the surface, magically turning everything around it lush and green. Springs feed creeks, streams, and rivers, and nourish and sustain plant and animal life. Springs are why Texas has been inhabited for tens of thousands of years.

Compared to escarpments, aquifers, uplifts, domes, valley, mesas, sky islands, estuaries, and the other natural attributes that make Texas Texas, springs are fairly easy to appreciate and understand. Almost everyone knows springs create swimming holes, and in the middle of a blazing midsummer's heatwave, there is no better place to be outdoors than in a flowing pool of cool, clear, spring-fed water. It's God's own air-conditioning.

Texas is blessed with several thousand springs, considerably less than before this region was settled two hundred years ago, perhaps, but more than just about anywhere else. Springs are found from the Piney

Woods of East Texas all the way to tucked away places in the desolate desert borderlands of far West Texas. The greatest concentration are clustered in that surreal landscape known as the Texas Hill Country, the proverbial Country of Eleven Hundred Springs at the crossroads of America, where coast meets mountains, prairie dissolves into tropics, woodlands transition into desert, and where wet and dry do an eternal tango.

Springs are people friendly. Humans have lived continuously around San Marcos Springs, the second largest springs in Texas, for the past 14,000 years or so. Springs were the landmarks that established seasonal routes for nomadic peoples who roamed this range for hundreds of years and for trade routes crossing the region. Springs determined the historic trails taken by explorers and adventurers, pioneers and fortune-seekers, and railroads and highways over the last couple centuries. For the past few generations, springs have provided aesthetic satisfaction for lollygaggers seeking a direct connection to Mother Nature.

I fall into that last category. Springs are my personal connection to the natural world, Texas or otherwise. You can have your Colorado mountains, your slices of watermelon and your gallons of iced tea. You may prefer passing as many of your waking hours in climates far away from here or sealed in climate-controlled comfort 24/7, courtesy of 50,000 BTUs of refrigerated air. I face the heat gladly as long as I'm close to a spring-fed swimming hole. That endless string of broiling days and sweltering nights that wear down the spirit and sap the want-to and can-do in even the hardiest of souls—that's my favorite time of the year. Springs are the reason why.

Oh, I'll tolerate a swimming pool in a pinch. But whenever I do, I'm reminded why Jed Clampett and television family on *The Beverly Hillbillies* derisively referred to pools as "cement ponds." It ain't natural. The chemical scent and sting of chlorine neutralize any sensations of being cradled in the bosom of Mother Nature, much less the natural world. Doing laps in a pool is about as satisfying as getting stuck in rush hour traffic on the Stemmons Expressway; the best I can do is stay in my lane and hope I don't lose count of the number of laps I have to do before I'm done. Charting my own course across a swimming hole is more like a Sunday drive on a meandering Farm to Market Road. In other words, it don't mean a thing if it ain't got a spring.

Great spring-fed swimming holes run the gamut from wild and unsullied to tamed and civilized. All of them promise a setting in which one can cool off, cool down, and cultivate the lazy streak that resides within us all.

The spring-fed swimming hole is church. To splash in water that is clean and clear and surrounded by tall, stately shade trees with at least one big rock to lie out on and jump off of, and a rope swing hanging from a limb is compelling evidence there's a higher power.

Especially in Texas.

It took two years of coaxing from my girlfriend to adjust to the chilly waters of Barton Springs in Austin to get hooked on swimming-hole swimming.

Then, one warm Saturday in October, my friend Ben Mandelson from Great Britain who had passed the better part of a year in Austin, turned me on to swimming in the offseason. Summer in Austin didn't end when Labor Day rolled around. In fact, with the coconut oil crowd gone until May, Barton practically became my own private retreat.

I was proud of myself the first time I swam the width of Barton, maybe 100 yards there and back. Then I did a full length, an eighth of the mile there and back. Before I realized it, I was hooked. Slowly but surely, I worked up to a quarter mile, a half mile, then a mile. I bought goggles, ear plugs, and a cap to keep my head insulated. No matter how far I swam, if I stayed in for at least 15 minutes, I'd get lost in this zen-like zone where I lost all sense of time and place (though never to the point of not occasionally lifting my head above water to watch out for oncoming swimmers). It got to the point if I didn't have my swim on a given day, I'd get cranky.

I started hanging around with the year-round swimmers who are informally known as the polar bears. With my swim cap, the 68-degree water would actually feel warm on a sunny 60-degree day in January, quite a contrast to the icy cold sensation during the middle of summer, which always dredged up the faded childhood memory of sticking my hand in a tub of watermelons floating in ice at Buddie's grocery until my hand hurt.

Prime time was early in the morning before nine when admission started being charged. I became familiar with the regulars who came every day, most of them elderly folks who after awhile convinced me they had found Ponce De Leon's Fountain of Youth in Austin, Texas. Swimming kept me fit, feeling young, feeling alive. It kept me from the surgeon's knife for a good two years after I developed a fractured vertebra in my lower back. I couldn't walk without a limp but I sure could swim when I hit the water. Though my daily routine began to revolve around the pool, I eventually concluded swimming is not a social activity like golf—it's hard to carry on a conversation underwater—but more like communing before and after church with fellow worshipers. We all felt a sense of ownership and connectivity to the springs.

I developed a series of underwater landmarks as milestones for each lap—the springs, the steps, clumps of vegetation here, a drop-off there—and familiarized myself with the pool's residents including crawdads, tetras, a huge carp, several turtles, and an eel. I observed the nuanced changes in vegetation, in algae and clarity that came with rains, with dry spells, with the time of the day. I often practiced a ritual of swimming twenty feet down to the bottom of the springs and touching it if I could hold my breath long enough.

My girlfriend became my wife. Much of our quality time together was spent at the springs. We raised our two sons at Barton Springs, baptizing both in the chilly waters before they could walk. Sunday mornings at the springs were a family ritual. We tried to go whenever we could during the rest of the week too.

One Tuesday morning, after the morning lap swimmers were gone and our family and the lifeguards had the pool to ourselves, the Dallas Cowboys football team, coaches and staff took a break from summer training and came down to the pool. I think the coach, Jimmy Johnson, wanted to test the players' character because a bunch of macho warriors suddenly turned into sissy boys when they dipped their toes into the spring water. Three-hundred-pound lineman Nate the Refrigerator Newton almost broke the diving board when he went off and did a cannonball.

Barton was just the start of my springs fixation.

After writing about swimming holes on numerous occasions, discovering new holes almost everywhere I looked, and fighting the good fight to preserve Barton Springs against a tide of development upstream without much success, I finally moved to the Hill Country specifically to have better access to a swimming hole.

I credit the oilman Eddie Chiles for the inspiration. Chiles owned The Western Company of North America, an oil and gas services operation whose advertising slogan was "If you don't own an oil well, get one." I must have had water in my ears when I heard those commercials because I swore Eddie's pretty pitchwoman was talking about swimming holes, not oil wells.

So I got one.

Some people live where they live to be close to work, for the schools, or for the neighborhoods. I live where I live for the swimming hole. It's like I told the mother of a playmate of one of my sons after she asked if I'd moved for the schools or the kids. I told her I moved for me. A happy dad can influence an entire family, I reasoned.

My wife approves.

"For one thing, it makes you sane," she told me. "It improves your disposition. It keeps you from going crazy after spending all day in the heat."

My younger son learned to swim in the swimming hole. A teenager now, he's been honing his stone-skipping skill at the swimming hole lately, designating one exposed boulder as the "skipping rock" and an adjacent boulder as the "waiting rock," proving there's still plenty of kid in his growing teenage body. My older son has left home, but whenever he comes back, he spends plenty of time down at the swimming hole, as well as at Jacob's Well, a local hole of some notoriety about which he has developed a sense of ownership, much the way I feel about my swimming hole.

My sister tells me the secret swimming hole I took her to not too long ago was the highlight of a weekend that also included a chichi party at The Mansion on Turtle Creek and a movie premiere in Austin. My brother-in-law reports the experience made him feel "giddy" and reminded him of his Arkansas boyhood.

My swimming hole isn't really mine. I just bought legal access. To be honest, it isn't compared to Balmorhea pool in West Texas, which I consider the most delicious natural swimming experience in Texas. But my hole, charged by small springs hugging the riverbank a few hundred yards upstream, has its charms. It is clean enough to attract squadrons of dragonflies and to test better than my well water. It is clear enough for visitors to be able to see minnows, tetra, perch (Texan for any fish small and brightly colored), bass, catfish, carp, and turtles in their element through the goggles. It is deep enough to swim about a quarter-mile without interruption, as long as you watch for the boulders lurking beneath the surface. I feel a sense of ownership, and take pleasure in picking up the trash around it that litterbugs leave behind or advising motorists contemplating crossing the low water bridge that dams the hole up and contributes the constant soundtrack of running water to the setting.

My calendar revolves around my swimming hole. From early spring until late fall, I swim laps in my swimming hole almost every day. During the heat of the summer, two-a-days and sometimes three-a-days are not unusual. Morning swims are a better wake-up jolt than two cups of coffee.

There have been evening swims at dusk while surrounded by fireflies twinkling under the cypresses and bats fluttering overhead accompanied by the croaking chorus of frogs that have brought me as close to nirvana as I think I'll get on this earth.

Moonlight swims can be both romantic and spooky.

The end-of-swimming-season swims are tests of endurance, requiring a swim cap and considerable intestinal fortitude. Swimming after floods is not a good idea due to dirty runoff and the fact that snakes can't see you any better than you can see snakes in murky water. A New Year's Day plunge has become a small ritual, but nuts nonetheless.

When it's too cold to swim, I paddle a kayak—another acquired taste that requires springs—or simply walk along the riverbank, remembering idylls of warmer days, anticipating the heat that will inevitably come again, and the cool waters that will soothe it.

Not too long ago, I went back to Burger's Lake on the far west side of Fort Worth, a one-acre spring-fed body of water that was the site of my first natural swimming experience. Burger's may not measure up to a Hill Country retreat, but it will do when the thermometer rises above 90 degrees. Almost half a century later, I was pleased to see nothing much had changed. The petrified wood cottage and the little rock building under the pecans and sycamores at the entrance still beckon like an elf's sentry at the gates to an enchanted forest. The high diving boards at one end and the diving platform near the jet fountain in the middle of the lake were still crowded with kids. The line to the trapeze swing was just as long as I remembered.

Obviously, I wasn't the only kid who liked the cheap thrill of swinging out, then into the water. Lifeguards patrolled the lake in rowboats same as ever. I didn't recall the chlorine in the water, but times have changed, I guess. What has not changed is that hundreds of people are willing to pay for the sweet relief of the swimming hole experience in Cowtown.

I couldn't help but wonder if at least one of those visitors I saw at Burger's will someday want a swimming hole of his or her own, too.

Even though I've got mine, I return to Barton Springs every now and then, just to check in and savor it as I once did regularly. As development has sprawled beyond the pool and the creek upstream all the way to its headwaters some 30 miles away, Barton Springs is more remarkable than ever. There are times when the water is so clear, it's as if nothing has changed in a hundred years. I have derived a great deal of pleasure watching friends get hooked the same way I did. Two recent converts I know begin their mornings at five a.m. in the springs, with downtown skyscrapers and the moon providing all the illumination they need in the dark waters. That's a little too extreme for me but they know like I know there is no better urban swimming hole on Earth. Period.

Barton Springs is merely one of many favorites. At the top of the list is Balmorhea, aka San Solomon Springs, a marshy cienega in the Chihuahuan Desert that was walled in during the early 1930s by the Civilian Conservation Corps. Balmorhea's 76-degree spring water is so ideal I have dipped into its waters every month of the year, sharing space in the winter with scuba diving clubs from as far away as New Mexico, Kansas, and Colorado.

Krause Springs, a sensuous swimming hole near Lake Travis west of Austin that is fed by springs emerging from an exquisitely manicured bluff above it that forms a waterfall adorned by maidenhair fern, may be the best-looking natural swimming environment in the entire state. Hamilton Pool, also west of Austin and fast becoming surrounded by subdivisions, is a placid grotto below a semi-circular limestone overhang that spews forth a 75-foot waterfall during wet periods. The contiguous parkland lining the banks of the San Marcos River as it winds its way through the town of the same name, below the headwaters of San Marcos Springs, is always good for a dunk, its transparent waters making for exceptional tubing and underwater viewing. The 1.5-million-gallon spring-fed pool at the Landa Park Aquatic Complex on the Comal River in New Braunfels, is a compact version of Barton Springs without the crowds, fed by the biggest springs in Texas. A few hundred yards downsream is the Prince Solms Tube Chute, a cheap thrill ride that inspired the nearby Schlitterbahn, consistently rated as the Best Waterpark in America, if not the world; Blue Hole in Wimberley, a city park along a narrow stretch of Cypress Creek with very cool, very blue water lined with rope swings dangling from the soaring cypress trees crowding its bank, has it charms. Anywhere along the Medina River between the towns of Bandera and Medina is a great place to swim. So is Neal's Lodges, a bucolic, old-fashioned family retreat established in 1926, perched above several deep holes along one of the nicest stretches of the Frio River, some deep enough for diving and swimming laps.

There are hundreds more like them, many of them known, some secret and hidden away like my swimming hole, all of them fragile environments that defy the logic of geography, geology, climate, and progress. Without springs, none of them would exist. Without springs, I would not be here. Without springs, I don't think Texas would either.

Attwater's Prairie Chicken, Kathy Adams Clark

CHAPTER 7

GARY CLARK

MEMORIES OF A PRAIRIE CHICKEN DANCE

Gary Clark is a dean at North Harris College and author of "Wonders of Nature," a weekly column in the Houston Chronicle. His writing has been published in a variety of state and national magazines including *AAA Journeys, Birds & Blooms, Birder's World, Living Bird, Rivers, Texas Highways, Texas Parks & Wildlife, Texas Wildlife*, and *Women in the Outdoors*. Gary's first book, *Texas Wildlife Portfolio* (Farcountry Press, 2004) is available through major booksellers.

Gary has been active in the birding and environmental community for over 25 years. He founded the Piney Woods Wildlife Society in 1982 and founded the Texas Coast Rare Bird Alert in1983. He served as president of the Houston Audubon Society from 1989 to 1991 and purchased the North American Rare Bird Alert (NARBA) for Houston Audubon in 1990. He currently serves on the Board of Directors for the Gulf Coast Bird Observatory.

During his collegiate career, Gary has been a professor of marketing, a faculty senate president, a Teacher Excellence Award recipient, and the Associate Dean of Natural Sciences. He has won five college writing awards. He currently serves as Dean of Business, Social, and Behavioral Sciences.

In the dawn light of a March morning in the early 1980s, I stood alone near a lek at the Attwater Prairie Chicken National Wildlife Refuge near Eagle Lake, Texas. Only a slight chill was in the air suffused with the fragrance of emerging springtime flowers like chickweed, prairie iris, and meadow pink. Fresh shoots of grasses like bushy bluestem, windmill grass, and eastern gama grass were dappled with dew, redolent of the scent of a morning bath. Meadowlarks began to fill the air with their piccolo-sounding tunes. It felt to me as though the prairie was waking up.

I was awake to witness an event, an ancient ritual, played out century upon century, dawn upon dawn, on Texas coastal prairies—the mating dance of the male Attwater's Prairie Chickens. I had watched the dance often in the years before, but I had also seen it become less and less common on fewer and fewer coastal prairies. In years past, I could have counted 1,400 birds—not many to be sure—in 13 coastal counties. A hundred or so might catch my eye on undeveloped prairies between Galveston and Houston, and I could count nearly 100 birds during any given spring on the Attwater refuge. They would fly up in front of me as I walked the trails through the prairie, and the males would stand proudly on pimple mounds near the trails surveying their territory. Even then, the chickens' total numbers were barely able to sustain a breeding population with sufficient genetic variability to be viable, and the prairies available to them were succumbing to urban development.

Quite simply, dwindling coastal prairies meant dwindling prairie chickens. A century and a half ago, the prairies stretched inland 80 miles and covered at least seven million acres of the Texas coast from Louisiana to South Texas, sustaining over a million Attwater's Prairie Chickens, grouse-like birds that are a sub-species of the Greater Prairie Chickens that once numbered in the hundreds of thousands on the Great Plains but are now drastically reduced in numbers. So plentiful were the Attwater's Prairie Chickens that early Texas settlers shot them for food with as little thought as we today pick abundant edible dewberries off roadside vines. By the late twentieth century, descendants of the Texas settlers had razed all but 200,000 fragmented acres of coastal prairies, leaving at the close of the century fewer than 50 prairie chickens on limited lands like the Attwater refuge.

As I stood on the refuge in the barely lit dawn, I wondered if I were standing on a vanishing stage waiting for a waning dance.

Soon, the dance began. Five or six male chickens strutted onto a nearby lek, a flat grassy patch on the prairie. They squared off, two at a time, like gladiators in an ancient Roman arena. The chickens, though, were not in the arena to maim or kill each other. They were there to intimidate each other with a dance, and to prove their prowess to a group of by-standing females. Still, the dance looked like a fight.

They stomped their feet rapidly on the ground with an audible thump-thump-thump that resembled the soft drumming of timpani (hence, the genus name for the birds, *Tympanuchus*). They lowered their heads and erected blackish-orange neck feathers that looked like horned helmets and began uttering a low-pitched droning sound that rolled across the prairie with a WOOOO-LOOOO resonance resembling the sound of air blowing across the top of a soda bottle. Suddenly, they began to charge at each other, running and jumping fiercely at one another, then prancing around each other, then drumming the ground frenetically with their feet.

The ritual persisted until the sun was full up in the sky because the males needed to show stamina to the females who would later select from among them mates of superior vigor. Two other males, probably young ones, practiced their dance off to the side of the lek minus the moxie of the other males. Not yet ready, these youngsters, for the grown-up dance.

For untold decades, we humans have dubbed the dance of the prairie chickens by the onomatopoetic word *booming*. And we have ofttimes, if not seasonally, mimicked the booming with our own ritualistic dances. Did not the men of the North American Plains Native Americans, sporting fantastic headgear—made of feathers—model their traditional dances on the booming display of prairie chickens?

Do not modern, young college men mimic—if unknowingly—the dance of the prairie chickens at spring break when they strut on the beach in brightly colored swimsuits playing vigorous games of volleyball while young women watch on the sidelines?

Somehow, in ways we may not fully understand, I suspect we have deep ancestral roots in the prairie. After all, human life seems to have evolved to some extent on an African savannah. Native Americans like the Sioux and the Comanche built their tribal nations on the prairie. Our nation surely evolved dramatically when pioneers settled the expanse of the Midwestern prairie to cultivate grain crops that became the "bread-basket of the world." The concept of a prairie home is ingrained in our culture. Consequently, I think I can safely wager that many of our rituals are modeled on prairie events such as the annual elegant booming of prairie chickens. I know I can safely wager that our way of life in coastal Texas with a tradition of robust independence born on fertile soil, abundant water, and plentiful wildlife is rooted in a prairie heritage. But I fear we do not treasure that heritage.

It's a heritage of wide-open spaces that early settlers saw as sweeping prairies from horizon to horizon because, except for the East Texas pine forest, Texas was mostly a prairie state in the early nineteenth century, devoid of woody plants like Ashe juniper (commonly called cedar) in the Hill Country and invasive tallow trees on the coast. The coastal area was a quiltwork of prairie grasslands including upland meadows and lowland marshes. Tree-lined rivers and creeks nurtured the prairie which, in turn, nurtured red wolves, cougars, coyotes, deer, and huge numbers of birds like ducks, geese, bobwhite, meadowlarks, sparrows, and… prairie chickens.

An irreplaceable part of the heritage was—and somewhat remains—the hydrology on the coastal prairie that restored ground water by allowing rain and overflows from rivers to seep slowly and cleanly into the water table, which had the added benefit of preventing destructive floods downstream. Also, prairie hydrology enriched the soil and opened up a bounty of grasses, flowering plants, and berries. Native Americans like the legendary Karankawa Indians, a group of nomadic coastal tribes, roamed the prairie to reap its harvest of berries, nuts, seeds, and to hunt its ducks, deer, and occasional bison. Rich soils and plentiful grasses allowed early settlers to grow crops and raise cattle, an activity that accelerated in the twentieth century to alter much of the character of the prairie. Seemingly endless open space and water lured cities and towns to grow larger and larger as they crept over the landscape with invasive shrubs like ligustrum and non-native lawn grass like Bermuda grass to erase all but fragments of a once vast prairie sea.

The bountiful prairie sea is no more. What now remains of the prairie accounts for less than one percent of grasslands that blanketed the Texas Coast from Baffin Bay near Kingsville to the Louisiana border near Orange. The grasslands have been fragmented by modern agriculture, invaded by woody vegetation, and displaced with housing projects and shopping centers. Gone the sweeping prairies, gone the red wolf, few the tall grasses, imperiled the prairie chickens.

A sad legacy of modern settlement may be the loss of a precious prairie heritage. Oh, I know that human progress leads to alterations of the landscape; moreover, I do not dream of prairies without cities and farms, although I do have nightmares about cities and farms without prairies. I do not want progress to lead to wholesale destruction of our prairies if for no other reason than that prairies sustain our way of life, as they have always done, by filtering rain water into the ground water, by nurturing the soil for food crops for humans, and by mitigating the effects of river floods downstream. Yet, loss of a prairie heritage means more than the loss a self-sustaining ecosystem. It means the erosion of the continuity of the human spirit, a spirit that yearns for the tranquility of wide-open prairie spaces with tall grasses that sway in the breeze, with wildflowers creating a pallet of glorious colors, and, yes, with prairie chickens that dance fabulously on the prairie stage.

When I stood on a remnant of the prairie two decades ago and watched the drumbeat dance of a remnant group of prairie chickens, I knew the drumbeat would become fainter and fainter in the years to come. Indeed, so faint it became that now, in the middle of the first decade of the twenty-first century, only 58 wild Attwater's Prairie Chickens are making a last ditch stand for survival on coastal prairies, and I can no longer go to see any of them do their drumbeat dance without careful escort by wildlife officials.

Fortunately, officials with the U. S. Fish & Wildlife Service are coordinating strong efforts to reestablish the chickens to sustainable wild breeding populations. Those efforts include captive breeding programs in places like the Houston Zoo, Sea World of Texas, and the Fossil Rim Wildlife Center with financial and logistical support from governmental agencies, conservation organizations, Adopt-A-Prairie Chicken donors, Tom Waddell Outdoor Nature Club, Boy Scout troops, and many other caring people. Adult chickens bred in captivity are introduced into wild chicken populations at the federal government's Attwater refuge and at The Nature Conservancy's Texas City Prairie Preserve; however, reproductive success among all chickens in the wild is marginal. Rarely does a chick survive beyond two weeks after hatching, despite fervent efforts to protect them from predators and fire ants. Causes of the high chick mortality aren't clear even to the best of wildlife biologists. Nonetheless, the captive breeding program offers hope to a species with otherwise scant hope of surviving another 10 years.

The best hope for prairie chicken survival is increased prairie acreage where chicken populations can grow in the wild to a self-sustaining level of at least 5,000 birds. Chicken numbers cannot increase to survivable levels as long as they remain dependent on two parcels of coastal prairie barely 100 miles apart between Eagle Lake and Texas City. One huge hurricane or a series of massive rain-induced floods—neither beyond a reasonable probability in any given year on the upper Texas Coast—could effectively wipe out the wild population of chickens clinging to life on those refuges. Indeed, massive floods in the mid-1990s were a major cause of the catastrophic decline of chickens from a population of 456 to a population of 158. But, if prairie parcels spread out from say Houston to Refugio could be set aside or at least managed for the chickens, the wild populations might increase substantially enough to withstand a local weather catastrophe. Conservation groups like The Nature Conservancy of Texas are working with private landowners toward that goal.

I wonder what Henry Philemon Attwater (1854–1931) would think about the plight of the prairie chicken named in his honor. Attwater was an Englishman who immigrated to Canada and later to Texas. As an avid amateur naturalist and one of the first directors of the National Audubon Society, he provided substantial data for early scientific studies of Texas wildlife, including the seminal work by Vernon Bailey, *Biological Survey of Texas* (1905). Attwater worked hard on conservation programs by promoting wildlife protection laws and specific legislation to protect the mourning dove that was being over-hunted in the early twentieth century. Were he alive today, I think he'd be a bulwark against the extinction of the prairie chicken.

Maybe the Attwater's Prairie Chicken will make a comeback because of the bulwark formed by wildlife officials, conservation groups, and private landowners. I hope so. I hope my memory of standing alone on a coastal prairie with the dancing chickens will be a memory one day for my grandchildren.

Yet, I admit to a degree of despair at the counter-trends of more and more concrete spreading over the prairie to hold more and more highways carrying more and more citizens, most of them ignorant of a prairie heritage vanishing to an ever-increasing array of instant-gratification homes surrounded by instant-gratification shopping centers. Shallow gratification in flimsy edifices may supplant profound gratification in abiding prairies.

Whether with hope or despair, my memory will not fade of that moment on a March morning years ago when I stood alone on a prairie lek to watch with unspeakable joy the wondrous dance of Attwater's Prairie Chickens. But as I watched them leave the lek quietly and without fanfare after their dance, I shed a tear.

Paintbrush and Fleabane, David Taylor

CHAPTER 8

MARIAN HADDAD

WILDFLOWER. STONE.

Marian Haddad is a native Texan, born and raised in the westernmost part of the state, in El Paso's desert town nestled between the Franklins. After traveling and living for periods in Boston, Massachusetts; South Bend, Indiana; and in San Diego, California, she couldn't stay away from Texas. Haddad currently and happily resides in San Antonio and adores the infusion of Mexican culture in this south central Texas city. One of her favorite pastimes is driving through Texas; one of her "most" favorite drives is the drive on I-10 to El Paso. She shares some of her observations made along this drive, as well as the drive to the Texas coast, in the following essay. Among Haddad's visiting writerships, workshop instruction, and poetry and creative non-fiction manuscript editing, she, of course, writes: her works-in-progress include a number of children's books, a collection of essays dealing with her Syrian-immigrant family that resided/resides in El Paso's bordertown, and two collections of poetry, one which deals with the landscapes and seascapes of Texas and Southern California.

I was born under El Paso's desert sky, "The Pass of the North," there, between the Franklins, The Organ Mountains; there, with Ciudad Juarez, Mexico, at my side; with southern New Mexico near me. I was born where three cultures sang, met, began their turning.

The arid places of the southwestern part of our state have always held for me a constancy, an open slate of possibilities. I remember living near Scenic Drive in El Paso; Father, Mother and I would ride up the long, slow-curving hill from our street at the foot of the mountain, our tires slowly crawling and curving up the hot asphalt along the rim of the road (and our city named that landing Rim Road) there, among the sun, the cactus and rock, there, looking out on our city and our sombrero-shaped Civic Center. The buildings down in that cavernous space between mountains the color of sand were important when I was five and six; I remember my father naming them in his daily list of things to do: El Paso National Bank, State National, Southern Union Gas, El Paso Electric, part of our place.

And so, whenever we'd drive up that road named Brown, up along the rim, I'd look to my left at the dry mountains and try to name the banks, the buildings, the streets that curved like snakes through our wide spaces. I'd look down and see the tall or wide buildings, their glass shining like crystal in our white sun. And there it stood, our Roman-like high school, proclaiming the name of our town, El Paso High: proud, and regal, and strong, there, in the middle of our city, like a coliseum with its grand pillars and many stairs. Most of us went to school there. The uncles, the cousins, the aunts, the siblings, and me.

And when we arrived at the top of Rim Road, we would always look out. In day, it looked wide and open and somehow endless, and safe. At twilight, it began its turning, its miraculous colors swooned out of sky, fire, fire, everywhere; red and orange-bronze, three shades of gold, molten fiery liquid sky. I would look out of windows to see this happening, great sky down. Sun spread like fire across our vast place; and the closer we came to night, dusk took on its regal hues: shades of blue, fuchsia, purples, periwinkle and azure, and then the deeper violets and amethyst. This is how the miracle would take its final shape for the night. We'd look out over the rim in our descent back down to our home, or up again, we'd look below us at the shimmering phosphorescent lights. They trembled and shivered as they stood, electrifying our night. City of lights, city of lights. There in that large, circular space between earth and sky. Scenic Drive. We would always take visitors along that way, silhouettes of cacti, yucca, and rock skirting the road that wound like a holy trail down through our night.

And sometimes we'd drive to Las Cruces, there in southern New Mexico. I love the name. The crosses. Something holy about this place. Old Mesilla: history, churches and stone. The long drive out to our neighboring city and state would take us by and through some farmland, cotton fields perhaps, through our El Paso upper valley, the long green fields, and if we drove up the interstate, we'd see this expansive sky, sun beaming through glass, our windows reflecting the light. A long open space from here to there, how close can two bodies be?

And we would arrive into the New Mexican terrain, and we would travel up flat roads where large wooden carts stood, filled with watermelon, cantaloupe, and truckloads of long green chili. I could smell their sharp, sweet scent in our air. We would bend sometimes, to pick some out of burlap bags stacked side-by-side, fill our own bags up, take the green bundles home, roast them, peel the skins slowly down, keeping the fleshy fruit intact, fill each with cheese, with beef, whatever we would use. And once we slid our trays of stuffed or unstuffed chili into our stoves, our houses would give off a wild scent specific to our place, our land, our missions, our space.

We neighbored close to that small town, Las Cruces, The Crosses… Old Mesilla, our neighboring spot, the square that held a church and shops and eateries, furniture chiseled out of wood, candles burning their scent through dry air, a gazebo in the middle of a small central park. The Double Eagle where so many of us would take our lunch, our coffee, our tea, a small theater that sat only two or three at tables while we watched films, ate sugared sweets, drank dark or light wine.

It didn't feel far from home. Our deserts bound us in their making, in our making. Land and earth and sky, the periphery of our place. We entered each other's cities like the houses of siblings. We always knew we were welcome, part of each other's space.

And maybe we would drive through Santa Teresa, the long dirt roads that took us out and up into a secret. Mountain Vista Road, its name tells of what we see. I stood and sat on a porch once at Casa de Suenos,

House of Dreams, twice or more, there, looking out at a dark, dark night; and across from me, straight across, I saw the long, winding trail I knew so well, lit up with white moving lights, Transmountain Drive, far, far away, but close enough to see, car lights peeking and shimmering down the curved road, they snaked down at a regular and endless and silent pace, lighting up that road between darkness, darkness on either side, a trail of steady headlights in their downward curving glide, inching towards me like a silent river flowing soundless through black night; and above me, the stars, The Big Dipper, the great constellations, clear in this desert sky, city lights so far away, and the river that runs through our land, and that river that divides Mexico from our United States, and the river that is so familiar to our place: Santa Teresa, Juarez, El Paso; this same river that divides two countries, somehow connects us. Water, water everywhere, a river we somehow call ours.

And the long drive back at night; if we were lucky we'd catch the setting of our shared sun. The liquid falling-down of sky, down to greet us, to paint us in its multicolored shades and sheets.

And if we had time, we'd veer left, on our way from our neighboring New Mexican state, back to our West Texas place—and if we had time, and if... we would veer up and into the majestic mountains of our westernmost sliver of state, there, up and up and up, we couldn't climb high enough in our cars, curving towards the light, where we would park and look out and down, crows swooping in and out of this cavernous space, the mountains at our back, the mountains to our right, to our left, right in front of us. The great mountains encircled us, proclaimed our night was here. Or coming. Whether the sky was orange and fiery in its setting light, whether it was purple or blue or sapphire in the coming on of night, whether it was black and lit electric with stars and stars and stars, it was *our* magical place—Transmountain Drive—Trans Mountain Road, we called it so many different things, but we knew MOUNTAIN was at the core of the slightly different names. We knew our mountains were holy and high and happening. Regal rocks that stood against a slant of a mountain wall, occasional brush, scorpions crawling in and under rocks, and when the wildflowers would bloom, we'd look down into a sea of canary yellow, sun yellow, fire yellow, liquid and bright and glorious. Wildflower. Stone. Wildflower. Stone. These are what we claim. Mountain. Sky. Sun. Moon. Night. Stars that shimmer in phosphorescent light. Even under our sun that heats and breaks and cracks the earth and sand, and even in our rough and sometimes much too dry land, *we are florid and fecund, we are the umbilical cord to the underworld, and the higher world, and the world floating around us.*

Come night sky, break, cast your many-colored light on our roofs, on the tops of houses, on our wild, wild, windy nights; sometimes dust mists our air, sometimes it does, and what is not beautiful about that? Sometimes I can feel small granules of sand on my face, and are we not made of earth? It reminds me of how sand and water make a body. Water. River. Earth. *We are dust and water / molded into flesh,* and this is the ground of our making.

El Paso del Norte, something holy about that. The Pass of the North, a place of passage, a place of entry, a tunnel through where we began, begin, continue to begin. Every day is a new white sun unfolding, sun so bright we cannot focus, sometimes we are blinded by this wild, wild light. No other sun like this.

And when I drive from my Hill Country place, and when I drive through the green, green hills and foliage of Boerne, Kerrville, Comfort, the central Texas space of water, water, everywhere, floods and fields and green and rock, and through cowboy prairie, Sonora, Ozona, the long dry place, occasional brush and shrub scattered between rock. A wildflower, a stone, sometimes appear side-by-side, or a field of flowers rushing by outside my window, unexpected in a dry field, and when the sun begins its late afternoon yellowing, after veering into Marathon, somewhere over The Gage, or back on I-10 driving by Fort Stockton, then I know I am halfway home, to the history of that place. And then I see the sun's setting in Van Horn, smoke-purple mountains in my rearview mirror, sometimes their peaks covered at the tip with snow; dry, cold wind against my face; air blows through an open window, and then the names I know, coming back: Marfa, the lights, Sierra Blanca, the grand snow-capped mountains, Allamore Hat Wells, Texas Mountain Trail, and there it is, intact, EL PASO COUNTY LINE, and then the familiar names: Tornillo, 1 mile, next 7 exits. Fabens, 1. El Paso, 28. Clint. San Elizario, 1. And the lights begin their spreading out.

And then, there is the drive from San Antonio toward the Texas coast. Farther away from desert, the coming towards bountiful, beautiful water. Two edges of the world, two edges of the world. Desert. Water. Possible to have two lovers. The water calls me, and I'm feeling Mexico again— coming up on it. Coming into it. A third skin. Something in me leaps at the thought of nearing home. What is a country? I keep finding myself welcome and coming into different parts of the world. Entering the Rio Grande Valley. Poppy-yellow flowers flying by and past me, looking into my rearview, I drive headlong towards the coast. I am starving for water. I rejoice in sky, in sound, in sun. Life is full. Field of yellow flowers, bright as sun, under a blue-white sky. The clouds are lower here, coming closer to water.

Palm trees in wind announce this terrain, and the clouds *are* lower here. And I *am* near water. We are mostly water—and so—when water finds us—or we—find it—there is no other healing. I have traveled through desert, the Kerrville hills, cowboy prairie, and now—this coastal sky—I revel in the roads and fields of this fine and seemingly endless state—Rockport in rain—Corpus Christi, body of Christ.

I am hungry and stop at Snoopy's by the water. This cigarette smells good here, in this coastal setting, and the gulls, and the two o'clock sun on these waters. I sit first, directly under sun, savor the burning of the light. And when that becomes too much, and when that becomes, I move inside, sit in a fairly dark wooden-floored room, still looking out on water, but the fan here breathes a cooler kind of air on my damp skin. Somehow, sitting in is not a satisfying place for me to be. I walk back out into a middle space, not the unshaded place of the afternoon's hard beginning, not in the cool inside air, but outside, on a deck, watching the light, the gulls, the boats. And here, a tall and graceful bird tightropes its way across the fat wooden beam of fence. The sun is almost touchable here, over water. There is a sea-breeze that flows cool under this awning at which I have found a place to write. I don't want to leave.

But then I go, back to North Padre's bay, Fortuna Bay, where I will sleep for two nights. Purple martins, blue herons, white egrets, and the oleanders, white or powder pink, bougainvillea, even a banana tree. John and Jackie on the boat. The clouded purple sunset. The pink swept sky.

After the boat ride, I climb a few steps to my balcony. I look out over the bay an hour before night. There are families in these houses across Fortuna Bay. I sit here, on a lamp-lit upper deck, reading, above water. Words. Water. The florid nature of them. And I look across the shimmering surface of what seems a lake—onto back porches, allowed to peek through glass houses. And so I seek the silences of night. Me, above water. The breeze is one degree from what I would call cool, but the air is balmy as salve, and the water laps and lolls at the edges of a boat, and the breeze sways this American flag more than gently in this night, and the stars dot this sky, somehow spread, as sky would have them. A mosquito tries its damndest to taste my skin, creature of this nearly dank, yet breezy night, and I revel in this silence, in this shut mouth, in no one taking my attention away from water, the boats, the shimmering surface of the water's light.

And after the night becomes as black as it will get, I move down to the pool and the large wooden deck. I lie on a lounging chair, looking out on what seems a sea. Almost meditating, I stare at midnight blue bay, the ripples it makes under moonlight.

Next morning, I leave the bay. Next step of the day, I go to the seawall, walk by the beach; though it is not as blue as I would like water to be, it is still water, and that is where I believe we were all born.

Mid-afternoon and I'm back at the bay. I am stretched out on a lounge chair and gazing at ripples, two feet away. I stare hard at them, and I begin my floating. It's as if the deck has removed itself, become a barge, and I am floating—far—far away—buoyed up and bobbing, transcendental meditation. I understand now.

Then evening in downtown Corpus: Shoreline, Water Street. These are the names that call me in. A desire for water—and across the shore, the lights: green, red, gold, and the lit towers. The breeze—blue nocturnal pulse—lights on a large boat.

Next day, at Port Aransas, the Dennis Dreyer Municipal Harbor, I see a woman flicking the scales off a fish. The fish is in her left hand. I hear the sounds first, a hard-type of shaving, like playing a washboard, the knife poised and firm in her right hand. She plays that scaly skin up and down. The sound of learning. And then she dips the fish she holds tight in her left hand into a large, white bucket of water, slightly red—darker than pink—as she swirls it around in the liquid. She sits—there—on the almost square, rectangular rocks that jag up or down in rows on this slight incline—legs outspread as she works—huddled around the bucket where she dips the fish's body into the bloody water, her head bent slightly down, over it. Her and her visor, her candy-pink shirt, khaki shorts, and the color—of blood. She is there, at work, in this hot Port Aransas sun. Fishermen. The piers are full of them.

And there, the large boats are gliding down one side of me; and over here, the tri-floor houses stacked, almost against each other, colorful in this light—one is peach; one, darker than coral; another, mint green. These are the colors of summer.

I ask a woman how to get to Rockport from here. She says I have to board a ferry. Me and my car. I am first in line, here in the middle lane, and I see the *B. L. Deberry* pulling up at the dock—Ramp 4—I have never done this before. All these cars aboard, lined up in rows, poised and ready to drive off after landing—taillights looking out at water. I can see the faces. And the state police overlook our driving out.

It's 4:40. Driving into Rockport. A little cooler here. More overcast. I feel as if I am in Massachusetts, not just because of the name. Water everywhere, and the palms swaying, leaning in wind, endless circles of water. Breezy. There is more movement in these bodies. Key Allegro. Fulton Beach. It's beautiful here. No wonder everyone is smiling.

And I sit on the long peripheral back deck at The Lighthouse Inn, a few feet from buoyancy. These waters are active. Rolling. Forward stroking, millions of invisible swimmers lapping the sea towards the shore. I see them now, invisible as they are—one arm forward, the other arm arcs, or a breaststroke. Bobbing. And the water hits the low wall, graceful in its breaking. And the wind here is high, and fresh, and blowing. This place is so large. And the gulls flying by.

Then the sad driving out. These waters seem endless, driving along the side of the sea. Seagrass sways in wind. And trees across from water sway in grace from the movement water and wind have cast on them. I'm not happy about leaving.

I come back into Corpus again, large body of water. I see the North Padre sign, coming back through—on my way to San Antonio—hard for me not to veer left, onto SPID, something about this stretch of places makes me want to stay. So many different Texas skies, depending on the ecology of the place. And a few miles out of Corpus, these planted rows, diagonal in their placement, speed by. They remind me of the valleys in and around El Paso, the tall fields; but these have a movement all their own under their cool sky.

I am 100 miles from home, and the sun bright and coming down next to Lake Corpus, 2 miles from Mathis, and still a ways to go. I'll be driving in the dark again. I can never lean out of day in time. I don't want to leave these geographies in their dancing. From the coast to here, riffs of sky and cloud and seagrasses swaying in sea-breeze—and then, before home, blue-green fields of foliage, and the sky is still coastal in the shedding or unshedding of its light. And before I know it, I am miles away from Pleasanton. To my right, off Highway 35, somewhere before 99 and Whitsett, I see a tall man, pressed jeans and creased, a black T-shirt, and the straw hat; in one fell swoop, he swings open a gate, and I cannot stop the looking.

Clouds to my left slide by an orange sun, masking the light. Behind me, now far away—Rockport, Port Aransas, Fortuna Bay and North Padre and its blue plumbagoes, Corpus Christi's shoreline at night. So much water. And this coming back to land—is solid. Earth beneath me and around. San Antonio 57. And the bridges over rivers. Atascosa River—Atascosa County. A beautiful name—sitting silent in its sibilance.

I never like turning the headlights on. I keep trying—flicking them into play—I turn them off again—try once more—not dark enough yet. I savor the last quiet shades of day. Interstates stitching one county to the next.

And so I try to find my place between desert and water. I was born in the arid flat land at the foot of the dry mountains, and the river there creates borders between countries. We are connected to Mexico because of that river. Rio Grande—Big River; it claims that Mexico begins where we end, at the other shoulder of the water, a skip of a rock away, and it is a thin body of water that runs through our town. Our desert has an unending open sky, the mystery of silences, stars are brighter out here—comfort of home—snakes that crawl in-between large crevices of rock, crickets and their chirping, sounds of desert, dust kicking up behind the wheels of a car, road stretching up or down between dry mountains. Arid land, expansive geography, and the night mountains encircling and cradling the city's lights. We are the other side of water.

And then the seas, the water itself, lapping against the boats, sheets of water glisten under sharp sun. Just looking at sky, I can tell whether I am in the desert or far away from that place. Something happens close to the coast and into it. I look up at this seaward sky, and I feel water reflecting somehow off of it. I know, depending on the clouds, or the occasional repression of light—I know by looking up—that I am coming closer to water.

Even in the desert, there is water, a river that runs in the middle of a city, dry and brown as it may be, all the way up from Colorado, funnels down into El Paso's terrain, and I think of Elroy Bode's childhood river in the Texas Hill Country, and I make that river somehow mine, translate it into my El Paso place, my Rio Grande, Big River, and I recall, from whatever sky I am under at the time… I recall…

> *I walked near the river that went beside our town… I was there in that place… I was alone in the two o'clock silence of our world…It wore a groove in me as deep as memory… it was the heart of my childhood.*

This is where I learned the importance of water, there in a dry place. Where I began to ask the questions of race, and countries, and borders, where I realized mountains do not have to be green. There is a paradisical place where mountains are purple at dawn, at night, and brown at day. I never knew how beautiful our dry, mountainous space was to me, until I left and dreamt nightly of sunset over the Franklins, of crows swooping in and out of our cavernous space; and it is in dreams that these mountains come back to me, in the absence of that light, of the great and endless sky that I have lost for a day or a night.

Then, I see water, almost drowning in it, driving over bridges in Corpus, water to my left, water to my right, water bleeding somehow into sky's edge, into space, water stretched out as far as heaven, as far as our eyes can see. I can tell the earth is a circle from here.

Storm Clouds, Wyman Meinzer

CHAPTER 8

WYMAN MEINZER

NATURE WRITER

Wyman Meinzer has been a professional writer and photographer of Texana for 25 years. He is the author/photographer of eighteen books since 1993 and is currently completing five more. His photographs have graced the covers of over 200 magazines. He is the recipient of numerous awards including the 2003 Star of Texas (along with John Graves) from the Gillespie County Historical Society. He is also a faculty member at Texas Tech University in the Department of Mass Communication teaching Special Problems Photography.

I have always admired the writing style of the pioneers and explorers from early day Texas in the voice of Marcy, Gallagher, and Kendall and although few if any contemporary authors employ such stylistic eloquence, the writers of yesteryear have impacted my writing and fascination with our wild and remote Texas for over 40 years.

It would be interesting to find evidence of my first creative written endeavor, perhaps having its birth in my preteen years, and for certain with a leaning to the outdoor genre. I have retained, however, some short stories from somewhat later years, I think from the tender age of about 13. Even now, when I reread them some four decades later, I see a rough style that in time would offer our Texas land and sky and experiences therein from a slightly different perspective.

Inspirational support for my early writings came from many sources not the least being sky, wildlife, weather, history and the ancient badlands of the Texas rolling plains. Having grown up on a ranch in Knox County, the land graciously offered an inexhaustible source of inspiration and energy as I explored the canyons and arroyos from horseback over and afoot. A region gashed by eons of wind and water erosion and furred over by a sea of juniper and mesquite vegetation, these silt and clay red beds offered fossil and geological wonders to fuel the fascination of my youthful mind. From observing the predators and the prey or from the snows of winter to the great storms of springtime, I raced tirelessly across the 27,000 acres constantly vigilant and absorbing through osmosis the life way of this ragged piece of Texas. From this wealth of humble experiences I seemed to have developed a voice of my own.

I have to honestly say that I'm not really a writer by the exact definition. Unlike many, I cannot produce significant material about any subject at anytime. Inspiration is mandatory or I will not waste my time nor that of the readers by tapping out a superficial collection of words for the sake of writing. Case in point was a paper assigned by my freshman English instructor at Texas Tech University in the fall 1969. Until about mid-semester I had effectively botched almost all of my attempts at the obligatory biographical sketches and other mundane topics and was feeling lower than the basement room in which the class was held three days a week. But a new day was dawning in this neophyte's writing career!

In retrospect I think that John Lightfoot, the instructor, was onto something when he gave the class a list of topics on which to write a two-page paper. Perhaps he was feeling the frustration of facing an unresponsive class or maybe he was simply bored with the standard time-sensitive topics (i.e. Vietnam war) assigned that year, but nevertheless I will always think that one topic was offered just for me: "An Enjoyment of Hunting"!! I was about to experience an epiphany!!! With a boundless love for the outdoors and with heightened energy and purpose, I wrote that paper with an intensity as never before. In apprehensive dread

I watched as Mr. Lightfoot stood at the podium and addressed the results of the recent assignment and quite honestly sat in silent disbelief as he informed the class that my work was one of the best freshman essays that he had ever read!! From that moment on I realized that indeed I had a voice on paper.

In this age of computer literacy, words flow in cyber space like endless columns of clouds in a summer sky but four decades ago my thoughts were scribbled on bits of paper, most of which had a tendency to disappear in the course of time. A few of these, however, did survive the chaos of youth and remain as evidence of the energy and purpose possessed in the formative years of one's early career. The lengthy if not superfluous descriptions of great weather displays or philosophical gibberish regarding the use or misuse of natural resources was a source of comical reading while on the other hand this enthusiasm is the same that has effectively sustained the energy that continues to fuel my writing today. I still laugh at some of my youthful meanderings but, too, I regard the sincerity of their purpose with a degree of reverence. Supported by maturity and hopefully a somewhat better command of thoughts, the sincerity today is as intense as it was forty years ago.

As a student of wildlife biology at Texas Tech University in the late 1960s and early 1970s I had no aspiration to further my writing endeavors beyond the obligatory research reports, or expand on some vague meanderings in response to a wrong doing, personal or otherwise. But quite significant was the willingness to frequently express my thoughts on paper, a voluntary response to the primal creative desire, a real milestone for a man whose youth can be best be described as quite rural, if not a little bit on the untamed side! In other words, I hardly fit the definition of a refined fledgling author!

Most authors that I know suffered through a window of experimental "rambling," for a better choice of words, before they could honestly say their niche was found. Except for a vast amount of energy devoted to a budding career in photography, I was no different from other authors and sought my inspiration in an environment of personal choice. Luckily that environment augmented the nourishment of three passions: photography, writing, and a life in the outdoors, the latter, no doubt, influencing the flavor of the previous two more than any stimulus encountered heretofore.

Unlike so many of this professional genre, the inspiration to communicate my thoughts in a somewhat creative manner was not derived from being in the company of fellow writers and exchanging ideas and technique, although this approach would perhaps have expedited the quality and volume of my work early on. On the contrary, I was always a loner of sorts and spent every available day afield gaining energy, ideas, and inspiration from those tangible experiences that often flourish in a big land and beneath an oceanic sky. Indeed there is something to be said about living in uncrowded places as the expansiveness supports a feeling of euphoric independence, an element I found to be essential in fueling the creative process.

In retrospect I have concluded that careers for the "creative types" undergo many phases, most of which tend to be ephemeral and some potentially lethal by way of short circuiting the creative drive. An example was that fateful essay assignment in my freshman year at Texas Tech and the ensuing words of encouragement from my instructor that allayed the fear to express myself with the written word. That one hour's exposure in class helped give me the incentive and self confidence to continue building my base as a writer. On the other hand, a highly charged negative critique could have easily squelched an already fragile aspiration. We all experience these moments of uncertainty. But also there is a window of time, measured often in months and sometimes years, when the appetite for creative inspiration is voracious, and a mode of creative absorption is achieved—where a mental reservoir receives material for a lifetime source of writing fodder.

Perhaps the most formative period for this inspirational enlightenment occurred from the fall of 1974 through the winter of 1977 when I decided to toss conventionalism aside and move into a remote area of the Panhandle-Plains region and experience once and for all the independence that had seemingly eluded me during the previous years of the late 1960s. I had just finished a BS degree in Wildlife Management at Texas Tech University and somewhat disillusioned at the prospects of having to choose an immediate career endeavor, I chose instead to take a sabbatical and live a life of solitude in a one-room half-dugout cabin with no running water or electricity deep in the canyon lands of the southern Plains.

By day I roamed over thousands of square miles of big ranch country, often seeing no one for days at a time, deriving a livelihood from the pelts of coyote and bobcat taken with steel trap or rifle. By night I listened to the hiss of a mesquite wood fire in the cabin hearth and documented with pen and journal a nineteenth-century lifestyle in a twentieth-century world. Scribbling this daily journal by the light of a kerosene lamp was my only attempt to preserve observations and personal experiences far removed from the average lifestyle of the time, for I knew this utopia of youthful excitement and carefree adventure could not last. Most of the written thoughts were descriptions of the day's hunt but sometimes they included the impression of a memorable sunrise or sunset or even the despairing occurrence of gale force winds, the prelude to an approaching winter storm. But of importance was the fact that I wrote and wrote a lot! Thus my voracious writing binge continued unabated during those months of solitude.

My writing inspiration was taken not from the actual profession of shooting and trapping animals, although I took great pride in my outdoor lifestyle, but instead being subject each day and night to elements that lend to an awareness of the natural state known largely to those who have spent months afield with few modern conveniences to distract from the conscience of a youthful, inquisitive mind. The wind, the light, the absolute silence in a star-filled winter sky, the hiss of a mesquite wood fire, the call of a single coyote in late night or the hypnotic flow of falling snow over the vast empty landscape; all of these elements exerted a strong and lasting impression on a solitary young man living the carefree life in a big land. Indeed it was a time of subliminal inspiration.

> *"The influence of the land and sky has shaped the lives, dreams and aspirations of Texans through the centuries. This is the nature of our Texas skies."*

From *Texas Sky,* by Wyman Meinzer with an introduction by John Graves. University of Texas Press, Austin, Texas.

Mequite, David Taylor

Chapter 10

Ray Gonzales

Tortas Locas

Ray Gonzalez is the author of nine books of poetry. *Turtle Pictures* (Arizona, 2000), a mixed-genre text, received the 2001 Minnesota Book Award for Poetry. His poetry has appeared in the 1999, 2000, and 2003 editions of *The Best American Poetry* (Scribners) and *The Pushcart Prize: Best of the Small Presses 2000* (Pushcart Press). *"Tortas Locas"* is taken from his collection of essays, *The Underground Heart: A Return to a Hidden Landscape* (Arizona, 2002), which received the 2003 Carr P. Collins/ Texas Institute of Letters Award for Best Book of Non-fiction, was named one of ten Best Southwest Books of the Year by the Arizona Humanities Commission, named one of the Best Non-fiction Books of the Year by the Rocky Mountain News, named a Minnesota Book Award Finalist in Memoir, and selected as a Book of the Month by the El Paso Public Library. His other non-fiction book is *Memory Fever* (University of Arizona Press, 1999), a memoir about growing up in the Southwest. He has written two collections of short stories, *The Ghost of John Wayne* (Arizona, 2001, winner of a 2002 Western Heritage Award for Best Short Story and a 2002 Latino Heritage Award in Literature) and *Circling the Tortilla Dragon* (Creative Arts, 2002). He is the editor of 12 anthologies, most recently *No Boundaries: Prose Poems by 24 American Poets* (Tupelo Press, 2002). He has served as Poetry Editor of *The Bloomsbury Review* for 22 years and founded *LUNA*, a poetry journal, in 1998. He is Full Professor in the MFA Creative Writing Program at the University of Minnesota in Minneapolis.

In his essay "The Place, the Region, and the Commons," poet Gary Snyder tells us, "The childhood landscape is learned on foot, and a map is inscribed in the mind—trails and pathways… going out farther and

131

wider." He writes about the perception of young children and how we carry a picture of the terrain within us, things we learn between the ages of six and nine. Snyder concludes, "Revisualizing that place with its smells and textures, walking through it again in your imagination, has a grounding and settling effect." I may have internalized the terrain of the desert at a very young age, but it was the unlocking of my creativity at age 11 that got the tides turning.

Trying to find traces of these maps, I visit the recently opened El Paso History Museum, a small building on the east side of town that used to be a steakhouse. Old habits are hard to break; I think, "Only in El Paso would a restaurant building become a history museum and still look like a restaurant from the outside." An exhibit of photographs reveals what the town looked like before my family came to El Paso. I stare at panoramic images stretched across the museum walls, and a line from one of my poems emerges—"The heart is a self-portrait." It is also a downtown street in a yellow photograph from 1916, buildings I never saw before they were turned over to the ghosts. I squint as I study the tiny carriages and Model T's an old camera managed to capture. That tower over in the corner. Four children trapped there by a woman who lit a torch in 1914. The heart is not a historian, simply an oxygen machine in the old hospital where I was born, the building rising tall in the other photograph. The first movement of my legs was the same as the other babies born that September day in 1952. The hospital is now gone, 32 drawers of unexplained cadavers bulldozed, without a report filed. The heart is a petrified tree hiding under the bricks of the growing town, branches that held sparrows and pigeons under an evening sun, where the man dressed in black first appeared, 1904. Blink closer. Right there in the huge, yellow photograph, he leans against the last cottonwood before it was removed, the public hangings banned from the streets, executions of Mexicans and Tewa Indians moved to the basement of the building cropped out of the photo.

The heart is the survivor of rewritten history. It is the yellowing image of return, another photograph showing a man wading in the shallow fountain in San Jacinto Plaza, wrestling or feeding the alligators kept there in the fifties and early sixties. The fountain in the plaza cascaded dirty water, rose above the crowd watching five alligators trapped there. They moved heavily toward the trash and food thrown at them, one or two crunching coke cans, no one from the city keeping the tormentors away. One year, they found one dead alligator with three arrows in its neck, finally sent the rest to the zoo. Downtown El Paso lost its monsters, replaced by hookers hanging around the bus stops when I walked by as a boy, searching for something to replace the alligators, waiting for the plaza to become a miniature Christmas village. The tall tree ignited in white and blue lights the night my parents took me to see Santa. I realized there was no such thing as St. Nick when the guy in the suit said something ugly to the little girl ahead of me, his impatience disappearing as I stared, thousands of lights and Christmas villages blinking into a city, the fountain frozen as the look on that Santa who noticed I knew what he was. I skipped my turn on his lap to find the alligators in the pool waiting for me to hang over the railing so they could respond to my movement, slap the water with their long, heavy tails so lights couldn't settle onto their moving mouths.

This exhibit also hides a clock behind a brick wall, its secret mechanism ticking since 1932. It has been hiding in the bank building erected over the old courthouse that replaced the saloon built over the adobe wall that survived the destruction of the first pueblo. I want to repeat that last sentence to myself because it is the oral pronouncement of border history, one culture on top of another, crushing and reforming itself to make a whole new civilization come alive on the banks of the Rio Grande. The layer upon layer makes me leave the museum. Before I go, I stare at another nine-foot-wide panoramic photo of downtown, 1918. The mud pueblo is somewhere underneath. I try to pinpoint it— right there, in the old photo pulled out of the archives where the heart does not belong. These close-ups of old El Paso send me away from the city and on a quick drive to the Upper Valley where the river erases the controlling smell of enormous, ancient photographs.

It was reported in a November 4, 1994, article in the *El Paso Times* that researchers have found that tequila reduces radioactivity in living things. Several scientists in Russia imported several gallons of José Cuervo tequila from Mexico and gave it to some survivors of the Chernobyl nuclear accident. These victims had lived hundreds of miles away but were suffering from radioactive poisoning over the years. A few gave birth to deformed children. The scientists reported that in some victims who drank several glasses of tequila, the effects of radioactive sickness diminished, though these patients remained ill over a period of time. They were weak, but their bodies showed signs of recovery, and some of the radioactive burns on their arms and legs disappeared. Further study was being conducted as the scientists awaited more deliveries of the fine Mexican drink.

I have driven along the Rio Grande hundreds of times, the river looking the same and often very different. It flows past a childhood of the desert and runs through my adult life elsewhere. As I cross the tall, yellow fields and head toward irrigation canals of La Mesa, I am only four years old and turning 50 this year. I count the years: 1999, 2000, and 2001. The Rio Grande flies by, its dark waters high and fast as they force their power under concrete bridges used by populations that come and go. When the Border Patrol pulled the illegal immigrant out of the river, his face was gone, having returned to San Luis Matalon, where the hands of the one he loved waited for him. What is it that won't wait for the Rio Grande's drowning victim number 17 for the month of July? How do we forgive the cracking mud between our fingers? The drowned man will never know how he made it home in time to become a terrible god arriving in the first flames of dawn, the dripping angels of blood and immigration spreading holy water over the town where Juan Melendez was born, then returned. The drowned man has seen it too often—the way the darkness interrupted his escape, the fleeing bats brushing his head as he drove into tomorrow, promising his family he would send money from the north. What fell asleep on the broken current and churned the crossing heart into sinking kingdoms of hope? How often did it hurt to open his hands and try to grab the barbed wire fence?

When a half dozen illegal aliens robbed a train west of El Paso in 1999, the railroad crew let them take what they wanted. The boxcars were broken open to reveal there was no food, only the heat of summer and 79 dead bodies searching for water, riding the tracks as if the train whistle signaled it was finally a new country. The Rio Grande kept its course toward the southern mouth of freedom, and there were 14 more drownings in the three weeks following the train assault.

What is beautiful but can't approach the water? How do we get it to come closer so we can all jump in and be swept to safety, our memories mushrooms to another life, the streets melting into the waterfall where every tribe that jumped in survived, until they staggered into the horizon with glowing bodies that could never be healed from too much water that sent them to a world of peace? What is this knowledge in the beating, swollen chest? How do we move to say we forgot it long ago? Who invented drowning and promised the water would always flow?

I drive for more than an hour, walk for one more, and don't want anything to come near me. I hike through the ocotillo field near Fort Selden State Park, then stumble upon the bricked wall of the public restroom and run inside. After I am done, I exit and look up. High in the darkness where the wall meets the roof, a cluster of gray bats sleeps and wakes, sleeps and wakes, their neatly folded wings resembling the pages I threw away when I tried to write the truth. What if I never go back to El Paso? Will the double agent of summer twist in the dry wind and reveal where the massacre of the pueblo people took place? I don't want anything to get in the way of finding what I have missed. A roadrunner has followed me into the park, its sharp head watching for anything that moves, the huge rattler that crossed the road not coiling in time as the bird strikes. Two of the bats open their eyes at me, their rat features in trance showing me how the man in danger comes out of the desert, slices open the barrel cactus, and takes a drink.

I pass the sharp ocotillo and salt cedars near Chamberino, New Mexico, and stop between two cottonwoods near the great bend, north of Hatch. It is the same, but the river and its trees have been transformed. As I drive across one of the concrete bridges near Canutillo, the broken adobe walls of two houses and the dancing graffiti on their mud slabs greet me. I am back and I am gone. I spot several boys splashing in the low water and can't tell if they are crossing, fleeing, or simply playing. There is no rain of white cotton from the trees that will outlast their friendship and outlive the torn buildings. I keep driving and cross, and they keep coming on.

The white rain from the cottonwoods kisses the salt of their skin, then floats toward the highway, their rivers meandering toward the other side where no one has set foot in years. The white cotton from the trees hovers across the arroyo that bends north, away from the Rio Grande, and keeps footprints on this side of the razor wire, away from the agricultural valley. Decades ago, someone bit into a whole head of lettuce from these fields and dropped the wet leaves here, the hard design of bitterness planting itself for the future harvest. The white rain from the cottonwoods keeps falling over the five abandoned buildings in the tiny town, whose name I do not know, the only street illustrated by black graffiti on the crumbling walls, one building proclaiming "Beware of Rattlesnakes." The white mist hits the ground when the locked door is kicked in and another rain becomes a forgotten road where adrenaline is an unlaced boot dragged out of the ruins by a silent tarantula.

I find the arranged stones in the middle of the clearing at the edge of town. They look like they were placed there by someone wanting to release something I should have freed years ago, but this person fled before anything emerged from the pattern. The smooth stones are covered in bright green moss, others marked in white chalk lines moving toward the center to tell me to pay attention. The stones were set this way to open the ground, not cover it, at least two dozen tossed yards away; the digger ran out of time as some of the stones rolled to replace what had been dug up. Then I saw the pattern emerge from what was left—eleven stones in the shape of a hungry dog, two the eyes of the carpenter who took the decaying lumber away, six others the rocks from a fallen sky that were shattered here to announce the church was built in the wrong place. It should have risen on the other side of the cotton field where the one stone of blue moss grows by itself, its roundness the top of the head of someone needing help standing up. My attempt at interpreting the stones that emerge from the desert soil forces me back to the city and an area whose stones are the barrio walls of family destruction and abandonment—histories surrounded by ruins and cemeteries where nothing rises, only disintegrates into hard ground where the remains of neighborhoods are as important as the desert.

The border guilt has to do with enjoying a wonderful breakfast in a Taco Cabana, one of my favorite fast-food Mexican restaurants in El Paso. I order huevos rancheros, the steaming rice and beans a great addition to the two over-easy eggs covered with hot sauce. I sip my coffee and enjoy the first good Mexican breakfast I have had in months, life in the northern arctic of Minnesota making it hard to find this kind of Mexican food. I take several bites and spot the boy. He is sitting at an empty table across from me, his mouth watering, his brown knees showing through his torn jeans. The Mexican boy has a starved look on his face and has been begging the few customers in the place for handouts. I have been too busy eating to notice him until he sits wearily, his mouth watering, his desperate eyes staring at my food. I stop in mid-bite and don't know what to do. I push my tray away and start to stand and reach for my wallet to give him some money, my guilt over savoring my food replacing the fine taste in my mouth. When I push my plate back, the boy jumps up quickly and runs out the door of the café, an employee shooing him out, my wallet frozen in my hands, the huevos rancheros sitting cold on the table.

In the summer months of 1939, El Sagrado Corazon Catholic Church in El Paso gave first confessions and holy communion to 3,812 Mexican boys and girls. Of that number, 1,456 are known to be alive, all of them in their early seventies. Of this smaller number, 1,014 still live in El Paso and 442 are scattered over the United States and Mexico. Of the other 2,356 people, death certificates show 1,759 are buried in El Paso cemeteries and 92 are buried elsewhere. The remaining 505 boys and girls who were cleaned of their sins throughout the summer of 1939 are unaccounted for. Their names remain on the archival rolls of El Sagrado Corazon.

That same summer of 1939, the *El Paso Herald Post* ran four different short articles on UFO sightings in the deserts around the small city. The first documents strange lights witnessed by several people way out on old Paisano Drive near the river. The second story, appearing two days later, talks about oval-shaped vehicles spotted in the skies over the eastern slopes of the Franklin Mountains. The third interviews a Johnny Cervantes, who says he saw several flashes of light near San Lorenzo, in the lower valley, and swears his car radio went crazy with the interference the night he sat in it and looked up at the lights. The fourth said the reporter could not get anyone from Fort Bliss to talk about the various sightings and listed a phone number of a local group of citizens who had been recording such sightings until one of their meetings was raided by military police, their scrapbooks confiscated, and the group shut down. Weeks of detailed examination of El Paso newspapers for 1938 and 1940 show not one single article about UFOs.

In the summer of 1892, seven mountain lions were shot in the Franklin Mountains after a rise in attacks on people. As the town of El Paso grew around the mountain, more of the wild animals came into contact with the growing population. In July of that year, six citizens of the town were attacked and mauled to death. The dead lions were displayed in San Jacinto Plaza, their thin hides and huge heads hanging from two trees for everyone to examine.

The old building in one barrio is closed and boarded up, indecipherable graffiti on its broken walls lighting the quiet south El Paso neighborhood. The rusting sign above the chained door says Tortilla Productions. Nothing else. No clue as to what they produce. Plays? Performance poetry? Comedy? The structure is large enough to house a small theater, but it is not the kind of area most theatergoers would come to at night. The boundaries for that kind of art are finely drawn in the border town. I cross the dirt lot bristling with broken beer bottles, pieces of old glass crunching under my shoes, ringing like tiny bells that want to lift their familiar sound from the desolation of the area. Next door to Tortilla Productions is another closed business, El Alacrán—Spanish for scorpion. The Scorpion Lounge—a smaller concrete box not only barricaded, but reinforced. The double front doors and the one lone window on its side are covered with iron bars. The graffiti on this ruin can be easily read—Tu Madre Es Una Puta! Then, an odd grinning face next to the pronouncement. Blue paint—the most popular color for tagging around here. El Alacrán Lounge. The sting. The bite. The night of the lone woman sitting at the bar. El Alacrán. The dark figure of a man waiting in the parking lot.

I cross the street to get away from the lingering odor of beer and piss, the fine layer of broken beer glass singing under my feet again, the rhythm broken by the sudden flight of two pigeons I startle at curbside. Their gray bodies flush into the early sunlight and disappear over the roof of the third decaying spot, Tortas Locas. It used to be one of my favorite neighborhood cafes. Tortas Locas. The funny name for delicious Mexican food that stung my mouth and filled me with tastes I have missed. Closed. Locas no more. The rectangular glass window surprises me by surviving abandonment. Long strips of heavy tape crisscross the window and make it hard to look inside. I peer through the glass, but the light won't illuminate the shattered counter and the two remaining stools, the others marking their disappearance by the holes in the concrete floor.

Suddenly, I hear the jingling horn of the Border Jumper, the new trolley that takes tourists across the border to Juárez. It is a compact motorized bus outfitted to look like one of the original trolleys that used to run on tracks connecting both countries before they became one. The Border Jumper passes two streets down from these ruins. It is a quick trip from the Convention Center to El Mercado in downtown Juárez. No one in El Paso has thought of creating a tour of devastated neighborhoods yet. It would be of interest to the wave of tourists that come here. After all, as I get into my car and move only two blocks east, I find La Paloma Café open— one of the best and oldest Mexican restaurants in El Paso, doing business before I was born, the old neon sign of a dove still hanging above the door. The tourist would love it, but to get to La Paloma would mean passing by Tortilla Productions, El Alacrán Lounge, and Tortas Locas.

They would not recognize the names of home the way I do when I leave south El Paso and drive toward Ysleta. Block after block of decaying businesses, most of them open and busy, crowd Paisano and Alamedo streets. Sign after sign of colorful lettering and advertising make me forget the Border Jumper. I pass the Viva Villa Bar, Dulcería El Loco, Azteca Motors, the Chicken Coop Lounge, Chilo's Radiator, Barrio Motors, El Yaqui Auto Repair, and Mina's Old Fashioned Hog Cracklings, then slow down in front of a laundry and cleaners whose sign says "Zoot Suits Available Here." I know these places. Their language has been with me since my first poem about the train and coyote. Llanteria California, Cuba Glass and Windows, La Salsa Income Tax Service, Arriba Bail Bonds, the Pink Flamingo Motel, Lobo Communications, and Taqueria La Pila.

In an essay on creation myths, Native American poet Linda Hogan says we are drawn back to our origins by the pull of cells in our bodies. No matter where we are standing on the earth, these internal magnets of biological connection implant the belief there is always a home and we must go there. In the El Paso area, neon and hand-painted signs are crucial in connecting this human yearning to the current state of our origins. Mr. Poncho's Hamburgers, La Milpa Tortilla Factory, La Malinche Mexican Food, Baldo's Haircuts, Castro's Fix Flats, Autos Mas, Yonke Auto Salvage. Signs of survival and creation myths with their visual effect—a key element in El Paso has always been the power of what is visually revealed in the surreal heat. These images call us to return in the same manner birds migrate and return each winter and sea turtles swim to the same islands to lay their eggs, generation after generation. A nest of advertising signs is a weird reason for migration; it sounds crazy. Yet this time when I read the signs and think, "Only in El Paso," I welcome the words on the billboards. Acapulco Bakery, El Escandalo Dance Hall, Salud y Vida Weight Control. I quit looking when I spot Home Sweet

Home Bank Repos. Hogan concludes, "We remember our ancestors and their lives in our cells. It is a deep and unspoken remembering." These memories are pulled out of the desert ground, their hidden profiles labeled with the alphabet of survival, poverty, and continuation—a lettering taken from English and Spanish to illustrate what has become of the town where I grew up, a musical alphabet that says more than a *Time* magazine cover ever will.

If writing about this place for decades means I am constantly recreating my home, I can leave and go north again, not be around when the last boarded-up building is torn down or too many of those wild billboards are erased. If years of failed and triumphant poetry blend together to map a new course for the river and the streets of El Paso, I have said what I wanted in my work, the hidden landscapes of yesterday finally emerging into the desert air. It is a gift and a loss. It is "history being overlooked" so I can live along the muddy ribbons of water and be able to say I wrote too soon, composed too late, and the twentieth century has ended. Yet my work was written at the exact instant the Rio Grande shifted course, the years it took for house after house and business after business to go up or down. I saw the river nourish its proud line of cottonwoods. I stood by the Great River and knew. Only then did I allow the trees to bend close to the water.

A Home, David Taylor

CHAPTER 11

NAOMI SHIHAB NYE

HOME ADDRESS

Naomi Shihab Nye's seventh and most recent anthology, *Is This Forever, or what? Poems & Paintings From Texas*, came out in 2004. "Home Address" is from her collection *Never in a Hurry: Essays on People and Places*. She lives in San Antonio with her husband, photographer Michael Nye and their son. Her collection of poems *19 Varieties of Gazelle: Poems of the Middle East* was a National Book Award finalist. Forthcoming in 2005 are *A Maze Me* (poems for girls), *Going Going* (a novel for teens) and *You and Yours* (poems). She is one of the many Texans who still believes in separation of church and state.

Yesterday we paid off the mortgage on our ninety-year-old white house on South Main Avenue. I drove from San Antonio to Austin with a cashier's check in my purse and a receipt marked HAND-DELIVERED for the mortgage company to sign. I wanted to see that stamp marked PAID IN FULL, to step back out the door into the sun and blink hard and take a full fine breath.

When I entered the marble lobby of the office building—cool and blank as any bank—beams of light were slanting through high windows onto the gleaming floor and the music playing over loudspeakers was the very same trumpet anthem I walked down the aisle to at our wedding fifteen years ago. I laughed out loud. It's been said our lives might be easier if we had appropriate background music, as characters do in movies. It felt wonderful climbing that staircase with trumpets to the second floor.

Later, back at home, I noticed all the cracks in the walls. They seemed more vivid. Now they were really entirely ours. We could fix them or not, depending.

My husband suggested we take a walk before dark. He and our son put on their baseball caps. I locked all the doors. We passed our neighbors' yards, thirsty after fifty-seven days of no rain. We passed our ex-cat Maui, who divorced us and moved five houses down to live with the Martinos.

An elderly couple dressed in white was crossing the bridge by the river, leaning on one another for support. My husband said, "Is that us in the future?" For some reason I jumped to say, "No!"—maybe because our son just started first grade this week after getting his first short haircut and losing his first tooth and the passage of time feels tender and nearly unbearable right now—but when we got closer to the couple, I figured we'd be lucky to be them.

They looked gentle, intelligent, and still in love with one another. He helped her into a white car and closed the door. Then he looked at us. He had a fine grin and a white mustache. "Nice river you got," he said. "You live around here?" When we said yes, he pointed to the River Authority building and said, "Well, I grew up on this very spot in a lovely brick house with a full basement, all erased by now, but you can bet I do have some memories."

Naturally I wanted to embrace him on the spot and urge him to tell, tell, tell. "The house has marble pillars," he went on dreamily. "And was full of music. We kept the windows wide open, so the music floated outside into the air. My whole family is musical; in fact we run the local music company, do you know it?" He gave the name. Everybody knows it. He said, "I wonder if there's anyone around here I still remember," and pointed at a tall white house. "Mr. Stump still live there?" When we nodded, he grinned. "A little crazy guy."

We said yes, he was right. Mr. Stump used to stop by our driveway and tell us he was being persecuted at work for being a white man. His mother wouldn't let him get married till she died. Finally she died and he married a woman ten years his senior who beat him. I kept thinking how he was one man challenging the status quo.

The music man said this river was a lovely place to grow up. He said some days his head was still full of "the scent of pecan leaves piling up in the autumn, right here, right along these banks. Look! There are some of the same old trees." He seemed reluctant to leave us, but his wife was getting edgy in the front seat alone. I would have liked to tell him about our mortgage or invite him to dinner. Where did he live now?

But they drove off and we crossed the river to come face-to-face with Mr. Stump, who didn't remember us for a few seconds. He gave us a fabulously suspicious look. He said, "I haven't seen you in twenty years." He was carrying a plastic grocery sack full of Miller Lite Beer.

"How's your wife?" My husband asked him. And he said, "Oh! She died last November. Gave all her money away to a cousin up in Kansas just before she passed. Can you believe it? I took care of her all those years, then she gives it away. I'm still recovering. I'm putting myself back together now."

We mentioned the old neighbor we'd just met and he said, "Oh yeah, the piano man, I bought a concert grand from him once. Did I ever tell you I got persecuted at work for being a concert artist?"

"Do you still have it?" I asked, picturing a concert grand inside his ramshackle house, and he looked puzzled. "Oh yes. Hard to give *that* away." He told us his life was wrecked and all his tools kept vanishing before his very eyes, but soon things would improve.

When he was out of earshot, I said, "He seems terrible," and my husband said, "I thought he'd never seemed better."

Next we noticed a neighbor's house for sale that hadn't been for sale yesterday. This always feels disturbing and melancholy to me. We found two frogs hopping around in the monkey grass by the sidewalk. Their rough little bellies puffed in and out. Our son said the frogs were husband and wife. They seemed to live under a raised cracked place in the sidewalk.

I could feel an ache rising up from the ground, a desperate deep thirst from the roots of trees and vines. In a few yards, quiet sprinklers swished in the darkness. "How much longer 'til it rains, do you think?" and we all placed our bets, then came round to our own block again and the iron gate that never fit the fence, even on the first day, and has to be shut with a shoestring.

Our porch swing was quietly hanging, waiting for us. A quilt top which used to be a curtain is folded in its seat now. I washed it once and the oldest fabrics came out shredded. The banana palms and giant red hibiscus bush were breathing their slumbered breath, and the black mailbox on a pole stood at attention even in the dark. Its flag was down. Now and then, each detail stands out like a landmark.

We sat for a while before going in and I thought of the lady who lived in this house for fifty years before us. She raised one son in this house too. She outlived two husbands in this house. Each time we invited her back for tea, she said, "Well honey, I just don't think I can make it," though the service station attendant around the block said he saw her drive by all the time.

I thought of Norman Bodet, who lived in this house before her, whose family built it and started the travel agency I frequent downtown. Bodet Steamship and Travel still uses old-fashioned blue envelopes with little steamships floating across them. Mr. Bodet's portrait stares gravely at me each time I buy a plane ticket, which is often. He seems to say, "Can't you settle down?"

The day after we paid off the mortgage I was sweeping the back deck, moving flower pots around and humming. I don't think I'd swept it all summer. I dug my hands into the big purple plant that flourishes with no attention. I plucked off its dry leaves. I pulled out twigs and the stick of a popsicle, tucked in by some lazy someone, and startled backward when something cool slithered past my fingers. Leaves rattled and shook. I glanced fearfully behind the pot to see a long snake gliding smoothly down between the boards of the deck. Since I only saw his middle section, I can't tell anyone how long he was. I must have waked him up inside his cool jungle hideaway.

He looked—mottled. Grayish or greenish or brownish. I've never seen a snake in this yard in fifteen years and now, the minute it's all ours, surprise.

He lives here too.

Paintbrush, Bluebonnets and Oaks, David Taylor

CHAPTER 12

GERALD THURMOND

FAITH'S PLACE

Gerald Thurmond grew up in San Antonio, Texas. He attended Baylor University and the University of Georgia and is a sociologist at Wofford College in Spartanburg, South Carolina. He has a fascination with all kinds of critters. He is an avid birder, he keeps snakes, and, as a sociologist, he is a professional people watcher. His essay "Midnight with Elvis" won the Hub City Hardegree Creative Writing Contest for non-fiction and was published in *Hub City Anthology II*. He edited, with John Lane, *The Woods Stretched for Miles: New Nature Writing from the South* published by the University of Georgia Press. "Faith's Place" was previously published in *Crossroads: A Southern Culture Annual* from Mercer University Press.

The white-frame house seemed much the same, but the little town around it was slowly dying. Old Calvert Street was mostly empty of traffic, and several of the stores along it were boarded up or had that hopeless look that empty, dust streaked windows give. I had traveled over 1100 miles to be here. For twenty years I had come, but now it was different. Now it was time to finish things, to fulfill a final obligation. I hesitated at the door, took a deep breath and knocked. A small, pleasant looking, gray-haired woman opened it.

"How are you, Velma?" I said.

"Well Gerald," (she pronounced it "Jurl"), "it's been quite a spell since I've laid eyes on you, come on in."

We sat in the small kitchen catching up, talking about the weather and drinking iced tea. Finally she said, "I guess you come to see Buck. He's in the back room."

I didn't need to be shown where. I had had a small part in the remodeling of this house, this second home that was meant to be a place of retirement from the country. But now it seemed wrong to me, its residents misplaced. I worked up my courage and walked into the room.

Buck lay in bed, bloated and white, unconscious as far as I could tell, but tended and kept alive. This big man, hands twice the size of mine. He had once knocked down a cow with his bare fist when his anger got the best of him. Now those hands lay beside him unmoving, or trembled and shifted aimlessly. I remembered how Buck and his generation once seemed to me as solid and substantial as the earth itself, as something I could push against. As I looked down at him the ground crumbled under my feet. He was my South Texas farmer/rancher father-in-law and I was his city-raised and mostly useless son-in-law.

I suppose my being part of Buck's life was as unexpected to him as it was to me. I met his daughter at the Baptist college we both attended, and after an on-again, off-again romance, when she was 19 and I just one year older, we married. She was blonde and pretty, and emotionally fragile like the smartest girl in high school often is, but also practical and down to earth too from her farming roots. Buck never said anything to me about our sudden marriage. I figured that he viewed me as one of those things you had to live with in a fallen world, a world where sinful desire often overtakes good sense. Buck's wife Leora spoke for the whole family, as she often did, when she told my young bride, "Well, I wouldn't have chosen him." I may have been legally part of the family, but I would have to earn my way into it.

To do that, whenever my wife and I would visit, I made a special effort to go with Buck to tend cattle, cut brush, repair or build fence, on what Buck called his "places." These places—no one but city people or locals with pretensions called them farms or ranches—were parcels of land that he either owned, like his Home Place, Fashing, and Choate, or properties he leased, such as McCoy's, Scott's, and the land that would become so important to me, Faith's. Some of the places got their names from the best remembered family that had once worked them—McCoy's, Scott's and Faith's were named after such families—or like Choate and Fashing were named after a small town that existed or had once existed nearby. If Buck said he was going to repair fence at Faith's and cut brush at Fashing and feed cattle at Choate, anyone in the family knew exactly where he was going.

Somehow during the first full summer of my marriage, tagging along with Buck changed from something that I had to ask to do to something that was expected of me. I took on my new obligation because I badly wanted Buck to accept me, and I tried hard to please him.

We must have been an odd-looking pair, riding together in his squat little International pickup truck. In summer Buck's face was brick red under his straw Stetson. He was over six feet tall and sturdy, with small deep-set light eyes, strong cleft chin, and broad, pitted, and lumpy nose that was as much the natural product of sun and wind as family line. When he took off his hat, because he wore it a little cocked to the side, there would be an off-center milk-white oval on that part of his bald head that was protected from the sun. When I said something to him about his odd tan Buck told me that the good Lord made just a few perfect heads, and the rest he covered with hair. I was a good three inches shorter than Buck and pale from the easy inside life as a college student. To protect myself from the sun I wore one of his old, beat-up Stetsons pushed down on my head, my hair, much too long, curling up under the brim.

Buck would drive along, looking straight ahead, occasionally inspecting a neighbor's pastures, or, without changing expression, he'd slowly lift his right index finger off the steering wheel to greet another pickup coming in the opposite direction.

To break the long silences of our drive I asked him anything vaguely agricultural that came to mind.

"Buck, what kind of cattle are those in that pasture?" I'd say.

He would peer out the passenger window and consider the question for a while. "Black Angus mixed with Brahma and Hereford, mostly. You want a mix, get better prices at the cattle auction that way. A little Angus makes 'em blocky, a little Brahma gives 'em vigor."

Although I was desperate to make conversation, for my own safety I tried to ask questions that only required a short answer, because Buck believed it was impolite to talk to a person without looking at him, even when, which was most of the time, he was speeding along at eighty or better on the curvy two-lane ranch roads.

"And, uh, uh… whose place is that over there Buck?" I said, staring straight ahead, trying to deflect his eyes to the oncoming tanker truck.

"Behind the Home Place is Faith's, ahead is another of my places, Fashing, and on the other side of Kenedy is Choate. That's the Scott's place we just passed, widder Scott is a good, Christian lady. Over yonder up that road is McCoy's."

As he drove Buck would read a man's reputation and even his moral stance in his fences. A serious, skilled, and hardworking man like Buck produced a barbed wire fence where the wire was stretched and taut, the fence posts level, wire on the inside of the posts from the road (if it was on the outside cattle could push it loose), with big, solid corner posts thick with twisted strands of wire bracing the posts against one another. For Buck, fences were an outer-sign of inner grace. Loose wire and an uneven, unsteady fence on a man's place were signs of a loose, unsteady man not fully engaged in the stern morality of work.

Steadiness of purpose was not only a moral virtue, it was a requirement for economic survival where Buck lived. His places were in South Texas along a rain line that divided a barely adequately watered coastal plain from the dry lands of the western part of the state. It was a chancy location for agriculture, and times had frequently been hard. This former prairie land had droughts of Biblical proportions, spells of five years or more when little rain fell, and men were forced to go deeper in debt to the local bank, or take their families and wait out the drought in some city, working at what they could, returning only after the rains had come back. Buck himself had been driven off the land during one five-year-long drought, supporting his family and his places by working as a welder in San Antonio.

In good times there was rain in late winter. Spring and summer crops were made if the rains were well timed; pastures were green and cattle fat, and there would be grass for winter hay. With rain a family settled its debts and paid cash for the new car, the refrigerator, and the sewing machine they had been putting off buying.

In dry periods rain seemed as random and undeserved as divine blessing, falling in spots, on this man's land and not another; while one farmer prospered the other had to plow under his crops; while one had hay and winter oats the other was forced to sell off his cattle at a loss or start a frantic search for bales. And all of this was a visible retribution and reward. In summer Buck could look over the low rolling hills and see the rain falling in the distance on some other rancher's pastures while his own cattle bawled for grass; or most cruel, the dark clouds would come rolling up over his land, the thunder would boom like the skies were announcing that his salvation was at hand, and then the rain would come in a useless spattering, evaporate in midair, or wait to fall somewhere else. It's a place where the Old Testament God, a god of strict requirements and capricious judgments, made sense. Buck probably wasn't the only local farmer/rancher who, in the midst of one particularly bad drought, carefully checked his tithe to the local Baptist church to make sure he had given the required ten percent. God, after all, was hardest on his own.

The best way to attract divine favor was skill, and Buck had that in abundance. There wasn't anything he couldn't do with his hands. He built his own house and barn from the ground up, he could repair any kind of engine, and he welded and created new farm implements and repaired old ones.

While Buck was blessed with practical skills I was cursed by their lack. That first summer, hard as I tried, I couldn't prove my worth as a worker. When we built fence, Buck's big Mexican hand Marshall could effortlessly dig two fence-post holes for every one that I dug with sweat and blisters. And tending cattle came no easier for me. One afternoon as I herded a five-hundred-pound bull calf into a pen, the animal gave me a sharp kick directly on my kneecap. I fell to the ground, rolling in the cow manure and dirt, crying out in pain. Marshall walked over to me, picked me up by my afflicted leg the way a child would carry around a doll, and bounced me up and down in the dirt to put my knee back in place, he said. Somewhere between the fourth and fifth bounce I decided that no kick in the knee was as painful as the humiliation of being dragged around upside down and I begged him to stop. One more bounce and he dropped me, the city boy, on my head.

By the next summer I began to get good at a few of the ranch chores. I particularly remember a morning that Buck and I worked calves at the Choate place. Buck put me in charge of the portable squeeze chute. One by one he ran the calves from the pen down a narrow fenced lane and into the chute, shouting at them and twisting their tails to speed them along. When the calf saw an opening at the end of the chute it lunged for it. I pushed the front lever of the chute down and two bars slammed, collaring the calf's neck. Almost simultaneously I pulled another lever that collapsed the sides of the chute on the calf and immobilized it. I quickly gave the calf a vaccination in its shoulder, pushed a yellow identification tag through the cartilage of its ear, and, as backup identification, cut a notch in an ear with shears. If it was a bull calf I castrated him. After I had finished I released the levers to free the calf. Some calves would scamper out, but others would be so dazed and confused that I had to quickly shove them out of the chute as Buck ran another calf in.

Buck and I were an efficient team and I was proud of what I could do. Of course there was still a big difference between us. By the time I pushed the last calf out of the chute I was smeared with manure, stained with blood, and covered with dirt from head to toe. Buck was as fresh and clean as he had been that morning at breakfast. He hadn't even broken a sweat. I told myself that this was only because I had gotten the dirty end of the job. So when Buck discovered that a cow suffering from pink eye refused to come up to the corral, and that he would have to rope her, I received the news with some sense of justice. After that cow had dragged old Buck through a good portion of a South Texas pasture he wouldn't look so damned neat. Feeling a little guilty for my thoughts I asked Buck if he needed any help, but he said no. In fact he seemed completely unconcerned about what he had to do. Buck went to the pickup, pulled the lariat out from behind the seat, and set off at a slow pace in the direction of the cow. He roped her with the first toss, and, before the surprised cow could run, he walked the rope quickly around a tree twice and waited. The cow bawled, and pulled and jerked against the rope, choking herself down until her eyes bulged, her tongue rolled out of her mouth, she wobbled, and finally collapsed on her side. With surprising agility for a man almost sixty, Buck leapt over the rope and treated the cow's eyes with medicine. In a minute he had released the rope and was walking towards the truck, still neat and clean, as the cow staggered to her feet. Then I knew. Hard as I might try, I'd never catch up with Buck's years of experience and bred-to-the-country common sense.

But I had become better at my chores and I wondered if Buck had noticed it. I received my answer one night after Buck and I had loaded a truckload of surplus lumber from a sign company in San Antonio. Buck had made a deal with some men at the company to swap the lumber for hunting rights at Fashing. I had spent the day putting posts and panels with fragments of smiling faces and cigarettes and beer and cryptic messages like Smoke! Enjoy! Drink!, all of which eventually would become the odd interior of Buck's hay barn. I had worked especially hard that day to please him. As my wife and I got ready for bed, I asked her, had she overheard Buck say anything about me as a worker?

"Well", she said, "the only thing I heard him saying to Momma was that you weren't very big."

My heart sank. It didn't seem there was anything I could do to earn a place with Buck.

Eventually Buck did accept me, but in a way I couldn't recognize at the time. One day we were driving toward Choate to check cattle when to my surprise he pulled off the road. I looked around but for the life of me I couldn't see any reason for the stop. Buck got out of the pickup and I followed him into a little country graveyard. The soil was chalky and our boots kicked up little clouds of white caliche dust as we walked. The graveyard was surrounded by brushy pasture: it was angular in layout, efficient in its use of space, Protestant and spare like most of the people who were buried there. To my young eyes the whole scene looked wind blown and forlorn. The headstones on the graves just gave names and dates, and by way of epitaph read simply "mother" or "father" or "wife of" or "husband of... son of... daughter of." One of the headstones stood out from all the rest because it had a crucifix above the name, one lone Catholic in the land of the Baptists. Only the nails holding Jesus' hands had come loose, and he leaned out, almost freed from his crucifixion, but held solidly to the cross by his feet.

Buck motioned for me to come over to some graves around a stunted hackberry tree. On the stones in front of me were the family names. He kicked at some dirt in an empty spot with his boot.

"See here," he said, motioning at his feet. "You can have this place right here."

This wasn't the sign of family acceptance I was looking for and it took years for me to understand. The matter of Buck's own headstone finally taught me the significance of his offer. When Buck's first wife Leora died of cancer, Buck ordered the stone with both his wife's and his name carved in it. All that it needed for its completion was his own date of death. For a long time, even after Buck married Velma, the headstone sat undelivered in his garage, so that when we drove in at night the car headlights would hit his name and the empty space for the date. Its appearance in the dark always startled me, but Buck thought no more about it than the headlights on the washing machine or lawnmower. For Buck death had its acceptable place, and finally I knew I had mine.

That didn't mean that things had become easy between Buck and me, particularly when it came to religion. I remember one summer

afternoon he and I were walking Faith's north pasture. He was surveying the field, trying to decide how to repair a farm pond (they're called
tanks in South Texas). I walked around the tank, and spotted something
curious on the ground. It was a limestone cast of a seashell. I turned it
over in my hand and imagined myself in the ancient shallow sea that
once covered the area. Then I showed it to Buck.

"Yep," he said, quickly handing it back to me. "Noah's Ark."

For Buck, church and his Baptist religion were one of the givens
of life, an extension of common sense: Coastal Bermuda makes good
pasture and good hay; mixed bred cattle are better than pure bred; every
word in the Bible is literally true; and a man needs to be saved, baptized,
and born again. It was living tradition for him. That tradition was a part
of me as well but a part I was trying hard to live without. Every Sunday,
morning and night, and of course Wednesday evenings too, the whole
family loaded up in the car and drove to the Baptist church in town. I
endured most of the service out of family obligation. However much the
preaching bored me, I still loved the old, brutal hymns that seemed to
match the land, and I sang them with pleasure.

There is a fountain filled with blood drawn from Emanuel's veins;
And sinners plunged beneath that flood lose all their guilty stains.

And

Rock of Ages, cleft for me, Let me hide myself in thee.
Let the water and the blood,
From thy wounded side that flowed.
Be of sin the double cure,
Save from wrath
And make me pure.

But when the inept emotionalism of the sermon began, I settled back
in the pew and counted the number of bricks in the wall behind the

choir, purposely confusing the count to occupy myself. I did this until the sound of the preacher's voice lost its cadence and leveled out, a sign that the service was almost over.

Buck must have noticed my inattention because he started to make up for the missed sermons by giving me a little preaching on our way to vaccinate cattle or string fence. One day as we were driving to Fashing he eased his foot off the gas pedal a little, slowing his truck down to fifty, and cut a quick glance at me. Then he began hesitantly, "Gerald... ya know... uh... the Bible says, 'whosoever will save his life will lose it; but whosoever shall lose his life for My sake and the Gospel will save it. For what does it profit a man if he shall gain the whole world and lose his soul?'"

When I didn't make any immediate reply he quoted some more scripture.

"It also says, 'Ask, and it shall be given you; seek, and ye shall find; knock, and it shall be opened unto you; for everyone that asks, receives; and he that seeks, finds.'"

I was a little startled to hear some phrases from the English of the King James Bible coming out of the sun-chapped lips of a South Texas rancher, and Buck's pickup truck pulpit call left me at a loss for what to do. Did he want a confession of faith? Or for me to ask Jesus to come into my heart—a conversion right there on the road to Fashing? I looked serious, cast my eyes down at my feet, nodded once... and let it pass. Having done his religious duty Buck did, too.

The truth was that I hadn't much concern with eternal life right then, and I didn't want to gain the whole world, I just wanted to possess the holy places that had been growing in my heart: Fashing, Choate, and especially Faith's. I knew by then I couldn't have them in the way Buck did. I would never have the skill to take his place. If I were going to be part of the land I would have to do it in my own way.

I started taking long walks on the places when Buck didn't need my help. At first it was usually just Sunday afternoons. Buck would be doing a little welding or other small jobs in his implement shed after church. I would come out the kitchen door and walk fast by the opening to the shed to avoid him seeing me. Because in addition to binoculars and a denim bag crammed with field guides and a canteen, I carried a little guilt with me, as if by doing something so useless as walking the land I was betraying Buck and his way of life.

Faith's was the first place I explored because it was so close. All I had to do was cross two pastures behind Buck's house and I was there. It wasn't anything special to look at, but it was a place of freedom, a spiritual place for me. Buck had worshiped his god at the Baptist church in town. Now I would worship mine in walking the brushy lands of Faith's.

The place had two fallow fields bordering it east and west, a rocky pasture to the north, and in the middle a little abandoned farmhouse on the side of a hill with two pastures behind it grown up in heavy mesquite.

At first I was no better at natural history than I was at ranching. I would cross into Faith's, spot some kind of a little brown bird or small plant, and spend the next 30 minutes hunkered down in the brush with my books, flipping rapidly through the pictures, trying to identify it, only to come up with the wrong answer about half the time. Or I would walk into the thorny chaparral of Faith's, get turned around, and come out in the wrong direction trying to get back home.

Over time I began to understand and feel comfortable with the land. I learned that if I walked out alone, attentive and quiet, I would see an animal, bird, or plant I had never noticed before, or see a connection between them I had never suspected existed. It was as if the land had chosen to reveal itself only to me.

On summer mornings I knew to walk carefully along Faith's

southern fence line because western diamondback rattlesnakes would be basking there. Along the dry creek bed and in the high grass there would be coveys of bobwhite quail that flushed before me. I came to recognize the different coveys of quail and I understood their habits and knew where I could expect to find each one.

Even the area around the old abandoned farmhouse had its treasures. Behind it cactus wrens would dart among the low brush. They wove conical nests in the cacti. I knew that they had one true nest and another false one to fool predators. In the open garage there was always a little screech owl that would fly from his roost to take refuge in the eaves of the house. Best of all were scissor-tailed flycatchers that nested along the fence line of the fallow field to the east. I would sit and watch them swing out from dead mesquite branches hawking insects in the air, their extraordinary tails, nine inches long in the males, spread, and their salmon-pink under wings flashing in the morning light.

In winter the flycatchers were gone, but there were more things I knew to watch for. Kestrels perched along the power lines by the road and did free-falls off the wire, talons extended, to pin some small rodent in the grass. A red-tailed hawk soared over the pastures, or sat solemn and still on the corner of the fence line, waiting for the rabbits that hid there. A northern harrier quartered the pasture to the south in low, swooping flight.

Sounds played a role too. I learned to listen for the low burbling calls of the sandhill cranes flying overhead. They are large birds, up to four feet tall with wingspans of five to six feet. I only saw them when they were flying high above me or when two or three of them were resting at a very great distance away in a field. Then one day as I crossed the pasture going to Faith's I was startled to see what seemed to be a great gathering of men near the fence. I lowered myself down into the dry grass and focused my spotting scope. What I found was a flock of sixty cranes, some of the birds standing erect, while others danced about, spreading their great wings and leaping in the air. And my mind danced with them.

By the third year I knew Faith's better than Buck or anyone. The land and its animals, even the cranes, had become commonplace to me. Now I wanted new discoveries. More than that I wanted to escape my lingering feelings of guilt. When I was walking Faith's I could sometimes hear the roar of Buck's tractor and catch a glimpse of his work shed from the closest field and all my old sense of uselessness would come back. So I turned my attention to Choate and Fashing, in part to escape those feelings. It was their distance from Buck and the Home Place that first drew me to them.

Choate was fifteen miles east of the Home Place, and was what most Texans think of as pretty land. It had open pastures of tall coastal Bermuda grass dotted with nockaway trees. Pecan trees grew along a small creek and, on the hill above, large live oaks with low, heavy limbs draped in thick mustang grapevines cast deep shadows.

There was more rainfall in that part of the country and it made all the difference. None of the other places had the large trees and the abundant grasses that Choate had and none of the other places, and few places in the whole area, had that magical thing, flowing water. It was a small creek. With a good running start I could jump it and in rainless summers it would dry up into a chain of slimy pools. But even that amount of water changed things. It had bass, catfish, and sunfish, we called them perch, and it had an abundance of water snakes. Exploring its banks I had to learn to distinguish the harmless diamond-backed water snake from the venomous cottonmouths. Most surprising to me, if I took one of the reeds that grew along the bank in my hands and opened it, often tucked inside was a green tree frog, its enfolded body shining like a recovered jewel.

I liked to end an afternoon ramble at Choate by sitting under one of the large oaks on the hillside. I would scan the pastures with my binoculars. Sometimes a coyote would cross the field below in broad daylight, stopping its trotting gait to stare arrogantly at me for a second before loping off into the next pasture. An odd long-legged bird the field guides called crested caracaras, but locals called Mexican eagles, would pace the pastures where the coastal Bermuda was low. No other place gave me the sense of peace that Choate did.

The final place I came to know well was Fashing. It was a good ten miles southwest of the Home Place and more than a mile from anyone's house. Almost a third of it was covered with thick, in places almost impenetrable, brush. It had two good pastures and two tanks, one of the tanks large enough to have a pier. The combination of brushy lands for cover, good pastures and water in the form of tanks provided ideal wildlife habitat.

Fashing was the first place Buck owned. Prior to Fashing he was a farmer, like his father before him, who made a living by tending other people's land. Buck had seen the stillbirth of a first-born child, a girl, and birth of his first son, while he leased a place southeast of Fashing near the little town of Burnell. His third child, a boy, was born almost nine years after the first son while they lived at Fashing. When the older boy turned twelve he wanted to play school sports and have more of a part in town life. Fashing was too remote for that. So Buck sold his house at Fashing to a family and it was moved to town. The money he got from the sale allowed him to buy the Home Place. He took the garage from Fashing, loaded it on a truck, and carried it to his new land. Later Buck, his wife, and three of his children would live in that garage for almost two years while he built his brick house, their final family place. It surprised me to think that Fashing held that much family history. Other than the corrals and the windmill, if you looked around you wouldn't find much evidence Buck had ever lived there.

I would drive out to Fashing, leave the pickup by the iron gate, and go up the narrow dirt road that divided the brush. I always looked carefully for deer tracks and tracks of the little wild pig we called javelinas in places in the road where the dirt was soft. Often a roadrunner would scurry in front of me as I walked. At the top of the low hill I would leave the road and turn north cutting through the mesquite, making my way towards the largest tank. At first there were wide openings in the chaparral, but the brush would quickly close in. Thorns caught on my boots and clothing, and at times I would have to bend over double to creep under the branches or turn sideways and push my way through the brush.

The mesquite would open up a little as I came closer to the tank. I would use it as a natural blind and scan the tank with my binoculars. In summer there were great blue herons and little blue herons patrolling the water's edges for frogs and small fish. Winter brought blue-winged teal and mallards that paddled about in garrulous flocks. After I had watched them for a while I would come out of the brush, circle the largest tank, and then follow a dirt road into the thickest part of the chaparral and explore the opening around the smaller tank.

I liked to end my walk by going back to the big tank and sitting on the pier. It was best to get there just as it grew dark. The first stars would appear. If it was summer and there was any part of a moon, I could look down into the reflecting pool and see water snakes, minnows, and water beetles swimming, their paths making a glistening calligraphy on the surface. I always thought that if I could someday read the messages they wrote on the water I would understand everything.

I stayed for a while to listen to the creaking sounds of the windmill in the evening breeze, the bawling of the calves and harrumphing of the cows before they settled in for the night, and finally the shrill barking of the coyotes as they called back and forth across the fields. Then it was time to go. Any later and it would be too dark for me to thread through the brush back to the truck without risking bloody scratches and the chance of getting lost in the thorny maze.

After those three years of walking Fashing, Choate, and Faith's, they were mine. Of course Buck owned them for all practical and legal purposes, but I held them for everything impractical and in bonds of affection. By then my wife and I had graduated from college and I was ready to roam. We planned to go away to graduate school in another state. After that we would come back to Texas to teach in some college and my love affair with Buck's places would resume.

It didn't quite work out that way. By the time we were finishing our doctorates the job market was so tight we couldn't even get teaching jobs in the same state, much less back in Texas. So we ended up in small colleges in the Carolinas, my wife teaching part-time, and we started a family. I continued to believe that everything could stay the same, and it did for a while. We visited Buck and his places on Christmas vacation and for a week or two during the summer, first my wife and I, and then years later with our two children. I still walked the fields. I still knew the land. But then it all started to change.

Those last years the land seemed always in drought. I would walk out into the pastures. The grass was reduced to colorless patches, trimmed to the ground by desperate cattle, and the ground parched and torn open in deep cracks. Even in the wild lands the grasses had withdrawn to the protective thorny borders of the brush, and there were fewer birds, less of everything. In these dry years Buck liked to tell the joke of the rancher who struck oil. When asked what he was going to do with his millions he replied that he guessed he'd just keep on ranching until it was all gone. Buck never acted discouraged, but he did tell his wife one long dry year that he felt like there were two little men sitting on his shoulders, weighing him down all day long.

Then Buck changed too. There was an accident. He stuck a tractor in a hole, and in his attempts to push whatever was available under the tires to get it free, a stand of barbed wire had swung out, caught his leg, and pulled it under the spinning wheel. After that he walked with a cane, seemed to have trouble with his balance, and eventually had to give up on much of his work with cattle. I thought that this was just temporary, and like the rains he would return, but he didn't. His trouble walking increased. There was something else wrong, but no one knew what it was.

My life had changed as well. I became more involved in my teaching career, and my wife went into working with computers and succeeded. Our lives became separate and too busy; it was harder to see what was important and what wasn't and more difficult to return home.

One of my last walks was at Faith's. By then I had seen Buck in time-lapsed stages of a relentless decline: Buck unsteady on his feet; Buck walking with a cane and having only a name, Parkinson's disease, for his ailment; Buck seated and silent; finally Buck sliding into a long merciless death imitating life. As I walked Faith's I realized how foolish it had been for me to have ever wanted to escape him. Buck's mark was everywhere on the land. He had created the pastures I walked in, the tanks I sat by, and even the wilder lands existed because Buck had chosen to leave them there. And I badly missed the days when we had worked together. I came to Faith's hill just as it turned dark. Across two pastures I could see the light in Buck's kitchen. The light told me that dinner would be ready, and more: that despite everything, I still had a place there, and that light would lead me to it.

Back in Carolina I had found another place to walk, a state park near my house, and I explored it with the same devotion that I had given to Faith's. And the marriage that connected me to Buck and to the family and its places died without my being able to say exactly when, although that death too was long in coming. I took frequent walks in my park; it seemed to me the one thing that had not changed. And I became charged with a simple conviction, expecting at any moment that someone or something would explain to me why things come apart. One late afternoon in winter I was stumbling down a ridge road when the misery of loss came upon me so powerfully that it knocked me to my knees. I remained there, head down, without the energy to rise, and awaited an answer. What I heard was the brittle sound of cold water falling over the rocks in the creek below, an empty winter wind pushing through bare branches… and nothing more. Another minute there: I stood up and walked out.

I stayed with Buck long enough to pay my obligation to him, said my goodbyes to Velma, and left. Buck never spoke to me or gave any sign that he knew I was there. He hadn't done that for anyone in a very long time. I drove to the edge of town and stopped where the road crossed the state highway. Suddenly I was angry with Buck. I wanted to shout at him, Buck, I looked, but I didn't find. You lost everything worthwhile in life and, God help me, I can't see that anyone was saved. Then I calmed down. Foolish thoughts. It took me this many years to understand that there is beauty and peace to be found in nature, even God, perhaps, but there's no message there, no answers swirling in the water, and no consolation in the parched earth. None is even pretended. And if there's hope in Buck's heaven, it doesn't explain, doesn't even come near to justifying, why a good man should die so cruelly. In the last reckoning, when the religion of the preachers has fallen away, and what seemed most certain and dear to you is lost, all that is left is faith, if you can manage it.

I paused for a moment at the intersection. If I went straight I could be at the Home Place in a few minutes, one more walk on the land I loved. Then I realized I was a stranger to the people living there now and I no longer had the right. I pulled out on the highway and turned east.

Elm Fork, David Taylor

CHAPTER 13

DAVID TAYLOR

PADDLING THE URBAN SPRAWL OF NORTH TEXAS

David Taylor grew up in Lewisville, Texas, and returned to north-central Texas in his mid-life. He has a beautiful daughter, a dog, and now has his own canoe; he tries to find activities combining all three. He edited this anthology.

Christmas holidays are for most a return. Whether that return is the ritual unpacking of decorations and the stories that follow, memories of a childhood Christmas, watching *It's a Wonderful Life* or *A Christmas Story*, or driving to visit family, the ghost of Christmas past pervades the Yuletide season. My own has always been a return to north-central Texas, to my parents' house. They live within eyeshot of the Lake Lewisville dam, and their neighbors across Mill Street are a small herd of longhorn which gawk and chew at the passing lake-goers.

At the time, I had lived in the southern Appalachians for almost ten years, first on the Tennessee side, then in South Carolina. I had grown accustomed to some color of seasons: winter, a definitive black and gray and dots of white in the high mountains; spring, full of a yellowish green and the fiery white of dogwoods; summer, still lush in cool rhododendron groves; and fall, oranges, scarlets, and yellows coat mountainsides fueled by what must be the poetics of a god somewhere. Such a god of seasons ignores north-central Texas, though; while spring is calculable by the reds, blues, and purples of paintbrush, bluebonnet, and winecup, summer is brownish-green; fall is brown; winter is brown and leafless. Landscapes are exactly what they appear to be here. Johnson grass leads you to no analogy or metaphor other than Johnson grass; mesquite is just mesquite; and the rivers are typically muddy sorts or a trickle running down a limestone ridge. This isn't to say that changes in the seasons don't bring changes in the weather; in fact, for my Christmas visits, I would pack warm, fuzzy pullovers and gloves along with the sandals, shorts and T-shirts. You just don't know about the weather. You don't ask for cool breezes too much during the summer dry months, and you don't ask for heat during blue winter northers. The problem is that that's what you'll get. The old adage goes for Texas weather that if don't like it wait around a while, it'll change.

Time with my parents often begins by watching whatever sport happens to be on TV, though we draw the line at any of those *european* sports as my dad calls them—soccer, games involving a racquet, or anything played on ice. Not surprisingly after a few days, this wears thin, and my brother, sister, and I each begin to venture away from the house. About this point, I usually call my best friend Scott for a beer and conversation.

Scott and I have a history near 20 years long, born of a match of well fitting opposites. He spent much of his youth in Minnesota, I, far south of there. Scott is tall; I am short. He can grow a beard and long hair within days; I struggle to compensate my enlarging widow's peak with something more substantial than a high school boy's goatee. For all my scattered energy and verbal harangues of half-born philosophy, Scott offers a somewhat placid and paced response. He allows his words to take their time and never once have I have seen him angry. Take, for example, the time we were fishing on a large cattle tank called "Moss Pond." We were three-fourths the way through a 12-pack of

Coors at nine in the morning and happily floated in the middle and cast large spinner baits into openings in the coontail moss. I remember distinctly the strangeness of my rod bowing back as I tried to complete my cast, an odd tug on my lure.

Funny, no trees, I thought.

Tug, tug. No lines or wires.

Tug, tug. After a minute or two of such poor reasoning, I heard Scott's voice in time with my tugs:

tug, "Dave,"

tug, "Dave."

"What Scott?"

"I think you've hooked me," he said languidly.

Turning around, I found that indeed I had, deep into his left shoulder blade, blood already dampening his plaid shirt. Even as I cut out the barb with my fisherman's all-purpose tool, Scott neither winced nor moved. Perhaps the beer, perhaps the drowsiness of morning, such a response is Scott, more pleasantly bemused than pained.

Adventures are born of boredom and energy, so this January afternoon as Scott and I talked over our lives now, of work and family, we drifted into stories of our high school days. Our stories were not dissimilar; each employed elements of eight tracks of Queen, Edgar Winter, and Springsteen, shag carpeting, adolescent experimentation, and hanging out by the lake or the river.

Lake Lewisville is the work of the Army Corp of Engineers, backing up Hickory Creek, Stuart Creek, and sundry other small drains, but its largest water source is the Elm Fork of the Trinity. The Elm Fork begins northwest in Montague County, is slowed to create Lake Ray Roberts, glides past Denton, and spills forth from the Lake Lewisville dam, winding its way to Dallas and below there meets with the West Fork to create the principal channel of the Trinity. Lake Dallas was the original lake, built in 1928 to be a consistent water source for Dallas and its northern suburbs; it was also called Garza-Little Elm for the Garza Dam. The same Black Prairie soil that makes fertile farming in the area, also causes siltation, so by the late 1930s and 1940s water capacity was drastically reduced. The Corps then completed the current Lake Lewisville Dam in 1955, significantly increasing the water storage and recreational opportunities for the wealthy of Dallas to work out their Freudian issues with boat envy.

During the '70s, access to the lake on the Lewisville side was free, so teenage gatherings were a nightly event. The flood plains below the Lewisville dam offered motocrossers miles of trails to wind and sputter down, and the river offered fishing and swimming. For those brave enough, Lewisville's version of cliff diving was performed off a railroad bridge, Scotty Tittle being the only person I saw attempt a front somersault. Scott and I agreed that the Elm Fork had played a part of our youth, but we had no idea what it looked like between the lakes. Scott said he had heard of someone renting canoes in Carrollton, and we both agreed the guy could probably use the business; after all, who would want to paddle the Trinity?

January 3, 1997
Elm Fork of the Trinity & 380
Denton, TX
10:00 AM

The day was a warm one, in the mid-60s when we launched. At the time, there was no easy access to the river. We had to pull off to the south side of the highway and leave the truck by a gravel drive and carry the canoe about 100 yards to the river. The access is used commonly by fishermen, and one sat near the bank, pole resting in the nook of a willow switch, driven into the mud. He reclined in one of those low, camping aluminum chairs, a styrofoam cooler nearby and by can count his third Bud already open, nestled in the mud. We nodded to him and asked about his day's catch. His return of "Not shit" and a big swig told us he was in no mood for witty banter. He watched intently as Scott and I waded the canoe into the shallows and deep mud to reach the channel. We each pulled our feet from the mud, making something of an indecent sound, and jumped in the canoe. There's an old song, "Texas River Song," that goes "Oh the Trinity's muddy and the Brazos quicksand." I sang a bit of it to Scott, to which he asked me to respect the fisherman's quiet time.

These were some big days for Texas music; on January 1st Townes Van Zandt had died from a heart attack at age of 52. His death was no shock to anyone who knew his music or him; friends said of Townes' death, "Ah, hell, Townes had been dying for years." *The Dallas Morning News*, *The Austin Chronicle*, and other papers ran nice biographies of him. People like to say of Townes that he was among the last of a breed of troubadour-poet songwriters—performers who loaded with nothing more than a guitar, three chords, perhaps four, and a raspy voice that could milk soul from the air of a room. Hearing Townes perform "Lungs" and "If I Needed You" could take an audience from lows to highs so fast that the club should have supplied seatbelts. Townes seems to have spun the yin and yang of his life just as fervently. In the darkness and light of sorting through his demons and angels lay a mental institution and the Colorado mountains, the colors of heroin and alcohol and the Cumberland mountains of Tennessee.

The only time I saw him perform a table full of rowdy jerks sat up front. They were the kind of group that if you go to listen to folk music often you already know—velour warm-up suits, endless chatter, hair from a bottle (men and women alike), cheap scotch and waters, a conversion van parked outside. Townes didn't strike me as the type to confront them directly; he looked as though he weighed about 160 pounds sopping wet; besides, he was already a few drinks to the worse. Instead, with no introduction, he began picking the A minor chord of "Marie." Anyone who knows it knows you can't keep small talk going during such a song. By the time he got to the refrain "Marie'll know I'm headed south, so's to meet me by and by," the room hung still and fertile. Townes could do this to listeners—take you to a place so dark and alone that silence is the only response. He followed with the ballad "Ira Hayes" and his drunken demise in a watery ditch.

The Elm Fork's water level depends entirely on the release schedule of the Corps from the dams at Ray Roberts and Lewisville. And rain, of course. Winter rains become a precious commodity for water commissioners during the summer, so the winter river levels are variable as lake officials stockpile water as rations. This time, though, the river flowed as it probably had before the dams (under moderately rainy years) with a steady but mild current. It is a good river to canoe on these days as traveling upstream is in no appreciable way more difficult than floating with the current. We decided then to head north a few miles and allow the current to take us back. Our paddles marked circles in the brown water, I, an engine in the bow, and Scott, our navigator in the stern. Slowly we began to slide along the gray-bone trunks of winter sycamore, shrubby box elder, pock-marked hackberry, and the deep-lined bark of cottonwood on the banks.

As chickadees flitted and twittered in the bramble, I told Scott what little I knew of Townes' complex but generally obscure story. His roots were Texan through and through—his family connected with oil, and generations old in Texas. Van Zandt County in East Texas is named after some ancestral patriarch, and there is supposed to be a Townes building connected to his family on the UT campus in Austin. Most liner notes and biographies of Townes emphasize his family's heritage and wealth; my best guess is that doing so gives his story the feel of church testimony—his high beginnings, his lows of life and spirit, and his inevitable return to the Nashville fold. His lows are the stuff of legend; bouts of depression so dark that Townes himself said at times self-mutilation seemed the best answer. His self-treatment included drugs and some heavy drinking dotted with bouts of drying out. By the time of his death, his alcohol dependence so great that DTs set in after only a day or two in the hospital. There were always the songs, though.

> *Down at the bottom of that dirty ol' river,*
> *Down where the reeds and the catfish play.*
> *There lies a dream as soft as the water.*
> *There lies a bluebird that's flown away.*
>
> *("Catfish Song")*

Scott didn't really know much about Townes' music, so I'd break into a medley every now and then. While I don't have much of a voice, volume is never a problem, and there's a good echo along the creek, sort of like singing in the bathtub because the banks along the Elm Fork are muddy cliffs mostly. The area from Dallas-Ft. Worth to the Red River is a jigsaw puzzle of three geographical belts: Grand Prairie, Eastern Cross Timbers, and Black Prairie. The Grand Prairie of limestone ledges, hardened soil, prairie grasses, and mesquites seems to bubble up in and around the sycamores, *bois d'arc*, and dark, soft loam of the Black Prairie; the post and blackjack oaks of the Cross Timbers surfing the borders between them. The diversity of soil, plants, and animals (what's left) is the culmination of this being beach property 60 million years ago: clay, sand, and black soil mark the sedimentary remains of estuaries, bays, and marshes. The Elm Fork follows the line of softer soil, so its banks are steep, slippery 10- and 15-foot drops with lots of erosion and exposed roots of sycamore and box elder. The angle of vision from the water benefits the aesthetic experience of a paddler; it's impossible to see beyond the short patch of forest left near the river. Thus, it provides the illusion that such forests extend far beyond their actual confines. Plowed fields or grazing pastures pushed within yards of the river—the water brackish-green on clear days and brown with sediment during rains.

Heading upstream was easy since the wind blew from the south. I churned with my paddle right or left as I grew tired on one side or the other; Scott steered by J-strokes.

"Do you miss it?" he asked.

I had left to pursue graduate degrees and the fool's gold of an academic life. I know people ask others if they miss their childhood homes all the time, but it's an odd question about north-central Texas. I might miss being able to see a Cowboy game with my dad or the lure of Dallas' Deep Ellum or the endless bonanza of shopping possibilities. Maybe I missed the myth of libertarianism that's a part of the West. The belief that long-hairs and cowboys can sit at the same bar and just let each other be. But missing such forgettable landscape?

"Yeah, I miss some things. Sunsets, open views. Mesquites, some-times," I said.

Scott never left here after high school. After finishing at North Texas, he had worked as a maintenance man at a summer camp in Argyle, then attended Occupational Therapy school at TWU. He and his wife Marjan have a house and three acres in Sanger complete with two boys, a few sheep, and a rotating crop of domestic animals; if a cat or dog dies another shows up to take its place within a week. It's mostly treeless (except for one large maple and the fruit trees they've planted) and very flat. Grasshoppers invade in the summer and leave the trees and garden bare of leaves. Though part of him longs for Minnesota, Canada, the Northwest or some other exotic place, he loves his land.

> *We all got holes to fill & them holes are all that's real.*
> *Some fall on you like a storm; sometimes you dig your own.*
>
> ("To Live's to Fly")

The Elm Fork meanders widely, swaying hard to the left and right according to soil density and slope. Dumping sites were a part of the scenery; an eroded cut-out making a fine landfill. Mattresses, old bikes, washing machines, plastics, and paint buckets were the notable items. Scott says this is the South's waste management plan—find a low spot and fill it up; we passed two on the east about a mile or so north of 380. We both grunted disapproval. A couple of buzzards circled overhead sorting out our intentions for what must be one of their favored dining locations. The temperature was now in the seventies and rising, so Scott and I, down to shorts and T-shirts, drank a couple of cans of beer we had tossed in the middle of the canoe.

"Well, it ain't the Smokies," I said.

"It ain't the Boundary Waters," Scott said.

I guess we're all given to this view of nature, that if it isn't "grand" as in Canyon or "great" as in Smokies, it'll do for suburbs, strip malls, and landfills. Especially in a place like this. I know that the growth and sprawl of the metroplex is in part due to jobs and economics and some of that other stuff I don't fully understand, but I've always held the conviction that one of the reasons it has bloomed humanly is that most of us deep down hold the notion that there really isn't a reason it shouldn't, no grandness or greatness to it. Nothing to preserve. Scrape down a few oaks and mesquites here and there and *voila.*

It's been this way since immigrants made their way here up the Trinity. The Cross Timbers provided shelter and fuel, and once the trees were removed the Black Soil Prairie made for good farming. It's a landscape that people think of for cash, not spirit or renewal or whatever else we think national parks give their visitors. I knew if I got out of the canoe and ascended the garbage to ground level I could walk the few yards of woods to a cow pasture. If I kept walking in a straight line east, I probably soon enter a fallow field, or two. In flood plains or fence rows I'd find some trees, but inhabitable places would most likely be inhabited. A friend tells me John Graves says it all about the region:

> There is a pessimism about land which, after it has been with you a long time, becomes merely factual. Men increase; country suffers… Islands of wildlife and native flora may be saved, as they should be, but the big, sloppy, rich, teeming spraddle will go. It always has.
>
> (*Goodbye to a River*)

I guess it's true; certainly it seems to be. I don't think the more rabid of environmentalists will come here and chain themselves to grasslands to stop another subdivsion. I know I won't; I'll whine and moan that it's all changing and practice nostalgia for my retirement years: "Ain't like it used to be," "Paved over that fishin' tank, you know," and "Kids got no place to get away these days."

> *It's legs to walk and thoughts to fly.*
> *Eyes to laugh and lips to cry.*
> *A restless tongue to classify.*
> *All born to grow and grown to die.*
>
> ("*Rex's Blues*")

The truth is, though, that I did not grow up in spraddle. Lewisville of the '60s and '70s was no outpost. It was certainly rural. Its population was about one-twentieth its population now, and when we lived downtown between '62–'67, I had chickens as pets, and the neighbors had goats and a mule. Possums, armadillos, even tarantulas were not uncommon; farmers grew peanuts, cotton, and oats only yards away from downtown; and once, when I was very young, our in-town church held a youth camping trip at the cattle pond just behind it. The next-door neighbor had a storm cellar we had to descend into when tornadoes ventured close, and almost everyone had a large backyard garden, full of squash, tomatoes, and okra. After all, the high school mascot is still the Fighting Farmers.

There was no wilderness to it, however, no woods primeval. The largest of forests I knew were most likely the scattered seeds of the mid-nineteenth-century deforestation. I have never known the Trinity as an untouched river, and my connection with it virtually always shaped by some human artifact: railroad bridge, dam, and the rise and fall of the current according to the release. The only non-domestic animals I was familiar with were those that had adapted to human interaction; if they couldn't, they were gone or about to be without intervention. I have always been at a loss to eulogize this landscape, when its wilderness was dead long before I was born. Too, I am not sure there is a language adequate to mourn the passing of marginal landscapes. I've read about the importance of saving wild places and the passion of its advocates, full of fire and brimstone, beseeching their congregation with descriptions of a heavenly places and jeremiads of doom. I have not heard a sermon for such slighted territories and don't even know quite know the words for it myself.

Scott said he wanted to go another mile or so to get what he could from the trip before we turned around; I started into another song.

> *There's lots of things along the road*
> *I'd surely like to see.*

I'd like to lean into the wind
and tell myself I'm free,
but your softest whisper's louder than the highway's call to me.
("I'll Be There in the Morning")

The most widely known quote about Townes is Steve Earle's liner note, "Townes Van Zandt is the best songwriter in the whole world and I'll stand on Bob Dylan's coffee table in my cowboy boots and say that." It's a big line, perhaps too big. Fans of Townes are like this; they speak of him in reverential tones. His music and songs are "gems" and "too good" for a commercial audience I've been told. Someone once tearfully told me he is the best poet he's ever read. Townes himself described writing one of his songs in an automatic writing frenzy—like thunderbolts from above—the words coming so quickly that his hands hurt. The words and melody to "If I Needed You" came to him in a cough syrup-induced dream. I too have toyed with the idea that Townes saw it all, telling me about my life through his songs of ecstasy and terror. Today, though, I wondered if we've done him a disservice in all this praise, missed something even more valuable than what is sublime in his work.

Townes responded to Earle's quote saying, "Hey, Bob Dylan would never let Steve Earle get close to his coffee table," and given Earle's current girth, probably a good thing for the furniture. Scott got a good laugh from that one.

"I wonder if they've missed his heart, Scott. That you can take just three chords, hell, D, G, and A for me, and write a song that's worth something," I said.

"What do you mean?"

"…that a good melody and a fine line, sung with heart and honesty is all it's really about for a musician like Townes. Maybe I've been looking at him the wrong way with all this sort of worship."

Scott waited before responding; he's used to this when talking with me because it's hard to gauge when I've really stopped.

"Dave," he said. "Over half of my therapy work isn't about stretching, mobility and all that doctor shit, it's about listening. Just being someone these people believe is honest as they're telling you their story about pain and hope."

I sort of knew what he meant. So much about Townes is about his eccentricity, not what's accessible and connected. Drunken sprees that still pass as heroic stories among the bars of Austin, feverish depressions that left him devastated touted as the necessary side effects of genius, but these build mountain peaks and awesome canyons out of the plain and simple art Townes could make. What's going on in his songs is just that, what's really going on: the story, emotion, and heart of a man being truthful with us about his good times and bad. I guess we do this all the time, make something exalted out of what's apparent and accessible. And then, because it connects to us, we'll make that connection something lofty—whether that be a landscape worthy of a park or an artist, especially a dead one. Maybe, Scott's figured it out all along, just listen.

Another mile or so up the river offered much the same, bend in the river, sycamore, cottonwood, willow, bend in the river, etc. We began to grow tired and hot; the wind was at our backs, and we knew the paddle back would be harder into the wind, though with the current. As we began talking about turning around, off in the distance ahead we spotted a bald eagle on a fine cotttonwood. I had never seen a mature one before, none anywhere near Texas. Scott said he had heard some were nesting on Ray Roberts. This, the first he had seen in Texas. Its sheer impressive size tipped me to its species.

I'll not lie that my first inclination was to make this scene a moral for something more about Townes, probably even something more about the Elm Fork, the remaining critters and woods, the spraddle of place preceding human contact 30,000 years before. I knew Scott anticipated this from me—something gushing and poetic, but being good friends, we gave it a quick "wow" and marveled at its wingspan in flight.

"Yep, an eagle," we said.

The paddle back included sweat, a couple of beers, and some swearing about the wind. An hour and a half up, three hours back with the current, but against the wind. I had given up singing, much to Scott's pleasure, and we talked little. I said earlier that most of Texas landscape doesn't lead you to make more of it than what it is. Maybe this is the reason so much good country and western and folk music comes from it: flat is flat; rivers are rivers; eagles, eagles. Anything sublime poets, singers, environmentalists, and audiences try to attach to it falls short of relating what it is.

Another Texas Highway, David Taylor

CHAPTER 14

STEPHEN HARRIGAN

WHAT TEXAS MEANS TO ME

Stephen Harrigan writes fiction, journalism, and screenplays. He is the author of multiple novels and collections of essays. He and his family reside in Austin, and he teaches at UT's Michener Center for Writers. "What Texas Means to Me" is part of his collection *A Natural State*.

Lying in a feather bed, in the guest room of a friend's two-hundred-year-old house in western Massachusetts, I suffered a lapse of faith in Texas. I'm not sure what brought this crisis on. Perhaps it was simply the act of waking up, looking out the window at the syrup buckets hanging from the maple trunks, at the banked snow glistening in the sharp air, and realizing that Texas would never be that.

I could stand to live here, I thought. I would keep my cross-country skis propped by the front door, a bowl of apples on the kitchen table, a steady fire by which I would read during the dim winter nights.

But it was not just Massachusetts. The hard truth was that I was getting tired of Texas and was now able to imagine myself living in all sorts of places: on one of those minor Florida keys where a little strip of land containing a shopping center and a few houses counted as barely a riffle in a great sheet of translucent ocean; in an adobe house, even a fake adobe house, in the foothills of the Sangre de Cristos; or perhaps in a city like

Los Angeles, which with its corrupted natural beauty seemed so much more likely a center for the development of urban chaos than Houston.

These were uneasy rumblings, and I was enough of a Texan to feel heretical in even allowing them access to my conscious mind. But my affection for Texas had gone unexamined and untested for so long that it was time to wonder just how much affection was there after all. There are certain people who are compelled to live in Texas, but I was never one of them. I am not a two-fisted free enterpriser, I have no fortune to make in the next boom, and my ancestral ties to the land itself are casual and desultory. Like a lot of other Texans, I am here because I am here, out of habit, out of inertia, out of a love of place that I want to believe is real and not just wished for.

Because I was born in Oklahoma and lived there until I was five, I missed being imprinted with native fealty for Texas. I don't recall having any particular image of the state when, on the occasion of my widowed mother's marriage to an Abilene oilman, I was told we were going to move there. But I did not much care to leave Oklahoma City, where my baby footprints were embedded in cement and where the world of permanence and order was centered. In the park behind our house was a sandstone boulder where several generations of children had scratched their initials. This boulder, whose markings seemed to me to have some ancient significance, like the markings on a rune stone, was one of my power centers, one of the things that persuaded me that I had not been placed arbitrarily on the earth but was meant to exist here, at this particular spot. In the same park was a little garden with a semicircular rock wall dominated by a bust of Shakespeare and brass plaques containing quotations from his plays. It was a place to ponder and reflect on the immortal bard, but its hushed and reverent aspect made me mistake it for a tomb. I had no real idea who Shakespeare was, only that he was one of those exalted characters like Will Rogers, and so it seemed perfectly appropriate to me that he would be buried in Oklahoma.

But all such reverberations stopped at the Red River. I filed them away, and with a child's tenacity I resisted letting Texas invade my essence. Abilene, Texas, had been named for Abilene, Kansas, and that fact was a convincing enough argument that it would be a dull and derivative place. Our house there had a dry, nappy lawn and a cinder-block fence. My brother and I attended a Catholic school that, in this West Texas stronghold of stark and bilious religions, was like a foreign mission. On feast days the nuns would show us Western movies and serve us corn dogs. Nearby there was a dispiriting lake where drab water lapped at a caliche shoreline, and on the southern horizon were low hills—looking on a map now, I see that are called the Callahan Divide—that I longed to think of as mountains.

But I surprised myself by being happy there. I liked the excitement of being rousted from sleep on summer evenings and taken to a neighbor's storm cellar to wait out a tornado warning. Though I did not know what an oilman was exactly, I enjoyed visiting my new father's office, looking at the charts and drilling logs and playing with the lead dinosaurs on his desk.

"Well, they sure do grow 'em tall down there in Texas," my relatives in Oklahoma would say when we went back to visit, and I began to imagine they were right and to cultivate a little my Texan identity. In my heart I knew that I lived in Anywhere, USA, that I watched *Crusader Rabbit* after school just like the kids in Winnemucca, and that my image of my own environment came from the same sources that everyone else's did: from *Giant*, from *Davy Crockett*, from a thousand stray pieces of folklore and merchandising.

But even this stitched-together notion of Texas had its power. Everybody else seemed to believe that Texas children were out there on the raw frontier, riding horses to school and pumping oil in the backyard, so who was to blame for us believing it a little ourselves? Even the false image provided a certain pride of place and left one more open for the real but impalpable expressions of the land itself. It became easier to imagine that the trim suburban streets down which I teetered uneasily on my first bicycle had been the setting for trail drives and Comanche raids. And there were other times when the land was almost unbearably evocative. Riding home at night from one of those Oklahoma trips, with the windows open, the car smelling of spoiled fruit, and the seats strewn with comic books and cracker crumbs, I would allow myself to become hypnotized by the way the headlights illuminated the barbed wire and mesquite on the sides of the road, creating a corridor, an endless bower that led us on but seemed never to deliver us into the land's ghostly heart. And then we would hit some little nothing town and the headlights would fall on the bobbing pump jacks, whose rhythms were keyed to a languid, eternal pulse that seemed to be everywhere, in the swooping wingbeats of nocturnal birds crossing the road, in the pistons of the car, and in my own heavy blood.

"I can see Abilene," my father would say when we were still fifty miles from home. "I can see a fly sitting on the window of our house."

"Where?" I would say, peering hard through the windshield, believing it was possible to see that far, as far as Texas went.

When I was ten we moved to Corpus Christi and I found that the image of Texas I had been cultivating and was now at ease with did not apply to this semi-exotic coastal city with its manicured bay front. This was not cowboy land. It was a sultry, complicated place, although the agoraphobia induced by the stillness of the ocean was reminiscent at times of the West Texas plains.

For my first six months there I was virtually felled by the humidity. I moved about in a tentative, purposeless way, like the anole lizards that wandered around the yard.

It was not a seductive place, but once you had purged your mind of false expectations and your pores of the last lingering traces of dry West Texas air, you began to feel accepted and absorbed by it. And of course Corpus Christi had its traditional charms as well—beaches and such—that the people at the tourist bureau seized every opportunity to promote. They kept shoving into the public view Buccaneer Queens and Miss Naval Air Stations, who posed seductively among the sailboat rigging for brochures that advertised "The Sparkling City by the Sea."

A ten-year-old boy could tell they were trying too hard, but I secretly wished the boosters luck. Corpus seemed isolated not only from the world at large but from the conventional stereotypes of Texas. It was not until the TV show *Route 66* deigned to film an episode there that I felt I had been provided with convincing evidence that the city was real.

I remember going to the courthouse one day to watch the filming of a scene. Within sight of this spot, Alonso de Piñeda had passed on his great reconnaissance cruise in 1519. On this bay shore Zachary Taylor had brought in 1845 nearly half of the United States Army and encamped while waiting to provoke a war with Mexico. On this very spot, perhaps, stood the makeshift stage on which Lieutenant Ulysses S. Grant had played Desdemona during a production in that camp of *Othello*. I was ignorant of all that, but there on the courthouse steps strode Martin Milner, and it was as if the shadow of history had passed across me.

There were not many moments like that, and the study of Texas history in the seventh grade served only to confirm my suspicion that the state seemed somewhere to have gone flat. Texas history began with Indians, conquistadores, pirates, with revolutions and wars, but by the time the student reached "Texas Today and Tomorrow" in the history book he saw only pictures of sorghum fields, refineries, and official portraits of dowdy governors.

So as time wore on and the universal ill humors of adolescence began to work their magic, I slid deeper into the down cycle of what I fear may turn out to be a lifelong mood swing about Texas. Corpus especially rankled and galled me. As a college-bound high school graduate, I had a clear shot at leaving Texas for good, but when it came down to actually making a decision about where I was going to go to school I threw in with thousands of other freshmen who chose that year to go to the University of Texas at Austin. The quality of education I might receive there never entered my mind. I liked Austin because it was an exotic place, where students rolled about on skateboards and wore surfer shirts and water buffalo sandals; and I quickly adopted the smug view that Austin, with its "cultural aspects," was not really Texas at all. The lesson I failed to grasp, of course, was that it *was* Texas, and that I had not really wanted out of the state as much as I wanted to believe.

That was years and years ago, and in all the time since, I have never made a conscious decision that Texas was where I was to be. Texas always seemed right for the moment, and the moments grew longer and longer, and here I remained.

Now I was beginning to feel that those years of dawdling and indecision amounted to a subconscious investment, that I had built up without meaning to a certain equity of place. That was one reason why the Massachusetts epiphany was so unwelcome.

I reacted to this crisis in a typically Texan way. I flew to Amarillo, rented a car, and took off driving. I had no plan really, just the raw desire to get out on the highway system and immerse myself in Texas. There were a few old haunts I wanted to see again and a few places I wanted to visit for the first time, but for the trip itself there was no excuse other than a self-prescribed saturation therapy. I was ready for the up cycle, ready to believe in Texas again, but I wasn't counting on that to happen. I had a vague apprehension that in some way I was laying it all on the line, that if Texas didn't "take" with me on this trip the clear inference would be that I really didn't belong here at all.

When my plane landed in Amarillo the man in the seat next to me nodded toward the window and said, "Pretty, isn't it?"

I'm afraid I gave him a rather blank look, because all I saw through the same window was a vast field of concrete and, far in the distance, the hazy Amarillo skyline, which at first I took to be a cluster of grain elevators.

"The weather, I mean," the man said, sheepishly. "The *weather* is pretty."

And the weather was pretty; it was a cool, capricious spring day, and every time the sun broke free from the ragged, thin clouds it seemed to deliberately spotlight some subtle facet of that monotonous land: the geometrical pattern of crops, the sight of black cattle against a field of frost-white native grass, the occasional swales in the landscape that were no more significant than the furrows between rows of wheat, but toward which the eye gravitated hungrily for relief from the flatness.

At a McDonald's in Amarillo I noticed a framed poster on the wall that told the story of the creation of the High Plains. God had been working on the Panhandle one day when it got dark and He had to quit. "In the morning," He said, "I'll come back and make it pretty like the rest of the world, with lakes and streams and mountains and trees."

God came back the next morning and discovered that the land had "hardened like concrete overnight." Not wanting to start all over again, He had an idea. "I know what I'll do," He said. "I'll just make some people who like it this way."

It surprised me how kindly disposed I was to this country. It was good land to drive through, though I could see what a nightmare it must have been to Coronado, day after trackless day in an unbroken field of nothingness. He and his men found some relief in Palo Duro Canyon, which to a traveler in that region is a startling rift in the plains, an opening into another dimension.

I drove through the canyon and was impressed but not overwhelmed. Texas scenery is spectacular only to Texans. Palo Duro pales beside the Grand Canyon, as the mountains of the Trans-Pecos pale beside the Rockies, as the coasts of Texas, its forests, deserts, hills, and even its cities, seem minor variations of grander and more definitive things in other parts of the country. Texas is a zone in which the stunning vistas more or less peter out, leaving us with only one great geographical distinction: size. The prudent and prideful Texan takes in the whole package while retaining an affection for the few component parts with the necessary spit and polish to be thought of as scenery. He develops an eye for breadth, along with an ability to look close and hard at the unlovely places and graciously accept them for what they are.

So I drove out of Palo Duro with a chauvinistic fondness for the place and kept heading south through the plains. Over the stripped cotton fields the dust rose almost vertically, and the wind riled the surface of the shallow, haphazard ponds that lay by the side of the road waiting to evaporate.

Soon the land gave way a little, and there was a miniature canyon where the Floydada Country Club golf course could be seen as a brilliant green strip beneath the eroded skirts of the mesas. After that, things were flat again for a while until the Cap Rock, where the ground buckled and broke all at once. Raptors suddenly appeared, patrolling the precipice. The change in the landscape was extreme and definite. Below the Cap Rock there were scraggly, alluring vistas, adorned with the supersaturated greenery of cedar and mesquite. That late in the season there were still beds of wildflowers, and soft, thick grass cushioned the banks of the minute creeks all the way to the waterline.

I drove through Matador, Glenn, Spur, Clairmont, and only then realized that I would be driving through Snyder, where my wife's parents lived. I came into town on State Highway 208 and passed through the town square with its windowless courthouse and its fiberglass replica of the white buffalo that had been killed near there in 1876. The buffalo was Snyder's totem, and though a drunken oilfield worker might occasionally knock a hole in the statue's head with a pipe wrench, most of the people I knew looked upon it with civic reverence.

It was dinner time when I arrived at my in-laws' house, and it went without saying that we would all go out to eat a big steak.

"How about if I order for you?" my father-in-law said.

"Fine."

"Bring him the Winchester. And we want an order of fried shrimp for an appetizer."

I ate three of these shrimp, each nearly the size of a potato, before the Winchester arrived. It was a big slab of beef, but I was hungry from driving and correctly calculated that I could put it away.

While we ate, my father-in-law complained with genial fervor about the state of the world. Since Reagan had been elected, he did not have quite so much to gripe about anymore. But even so, he had a few things on his mind. He was mad because the Democratic Congress wouldn't let the Republicans take a measly billion dollars from the synthetic fuel fund to stimulate the housing industry; mad because the British and the Argentineans were going to have a war over the Falkland Islands and guess who was going to have to go in there after it was all over with billions of dollars of foreign aid; mad because he had casually returned his YES token to the *Reader's Digest* sweepstakes and now he was being deluged with junk mail.

"There's something you should write an article about for your *Texas Monthly*," he said as we pulled out of the driveway of the restaurant, indicating a long-bodied motor home parked next to us. "These vans or whatever they are that block your view of the street when you're trying to pull out."

All of this good-natured grumpiness made me feel at home, and I lingered into the evening and finally ended up walking across the street to the high school with my mother-in-law to watch the production of *Ah, Wilderness!* that had recently won the state one-act-play competition. I was glad to have an excuse to see the high school where my wife had been a student, where she had edited the paper and written a column, under the name Sonya Stifled, complaining about the Vietnam War and the lack of paper straws in the cafeteria.

The production took place in an immense auditorium that had been built with tax money from the great fifties oil boom. The play itself was minor O'Neill but showed Snyder High School's drama department to superlative advantage. One or two of the actors even managed creditable New England accents. When the play was over and the audience was strolling out into the spring night, Snyder appeared less like a West Texas oil town than the idyllic Connecticut village that had been depicted in the play, a place with a tight matrix of tradition and community. It did not seem like the stifling place my wife had written about years ago, the place I might have glanced at contemptuously from the highway as I barreled through on my way to some hippie mecca in New Mexico. It seemed alarmingly like home.

The next day I got on Interstate 20 and drove to Abilene, finding by dead reckoning the house we had lived in more than twenty years earlier. The owners had painted it yellow and put a ceramic burro in the yard, and the neighborhood itself was largely shaded from the searing sun I had known there by all the trees that had grown up and over it in the last two decades.

It was all so comfortable and congenial: the creeks were swollen with bright ocher water, the streets were lined with upscale shops and the great Danish modern cathedrals of the Protestant faith, and the movie theaters were showing *Deathtrap* and *Conan the Barbarian*. I wondered if I was feeling warm toward Texas again or simply because it was familiar.

The land between Abilene and Dallas was unremarkable, but it held the attention of the practiced eye. In another month it would lose its verdant sheen; it would be dry and scruffy, and the very contours of the landscape would appear to recede and lose definition. But I had a fondness for that too, tucked away somewhere.

In this accepting mood I surged through Dallas in the shadow of the Reunion Tower, which had always looked to me like the centerpiece to a bush league world's fair. But there was no city in the country that was honed to such a fine edge as Dallas, and you could sense its organic singleness of purpose, its obsession to project style and busyness. You were either on the team or not.

I was on the team that day, and I drove confidently through the streets, enjoying the familiar feel of the city. Then I headed south on I-35, going through Waco and Temple and past a wacky entrepreneurial jumble on the side of the highway that included a crumbling replica of the Matterhorn. Then on US 183 to Lockhart, where I arrived in time to witness a reenactment of the Battle of Plum Creek. Bleachers were set up on the battlefield, microphones were planted into the ground. The epic, with its meager cast of dozens, required some thrifty state management. A Texas Ranger would ride in on a horse and announce, "I been shot by one of them dad-blamed Indians," and his mount would then be led off the stage, shuttled around behind the bleachers, and ridden in from the other side by a Comanche with a beer gut.

The pageant served less to bring the past to life than to make the present seem anemic and unreal. But Plum Creek itself, several miles away, had not been milked of its drama. It was Edenic, and along with every other creek I passed that day on my meandering way south—La Parra, Agua Dulce, Papalote—it had a lush, overgrown, hummocky quality that made you understand why this part of the country had been the fertile crescent of Texas history.

Even farther south, in the brush country of Jim Wells and Duval Counties, the land was surprisingly green, so much so that the dilapidated, boarded-up main streets of the less successful towns looked as if they were in danger of being reclaimed by jungle. Swallows dipped ahead of my car in relays, and turkey vultures and caracaras fed together on dead baby armadillos that had been struck down on the highway in their earliest forays.

A friend's father was being buried in San Diego that day, and I had adjusted my itinerary so that I would pass through town in time to attend the funeral. The church stood across the street from a zocalo whose gazebo and benches had been overgrown with grass and whose function as the center of town had been usurped by the highway a block away. Inside, the church was stolid and secure, its walls painted a light blue. Beside the altar was a full-color pietà, with dark red blood trickling from Christ's wounds and Mary bent down on one knee, holding her son's body in a way that suggested both sorrow and verve. It was a fine, grisly statue, with that admirable Mexican trait of being on square terms with mortal matters, a trait that was not echoed in the liturgically trendy stained glass windows bearing happy cubist depictions of doves and chalices and unsplintered crosses.

The congregation was dressed in suits and pressed ranch clothes. The service moved along in an unflinching manner, its bone-deep rituals making death seem real but not necessarily final.

I got back into my car feeling sobered and transient, a little flicker of movement on the landscape. But soon enough my attention was drawn outward again. The country was full of arresting things, from the painted bunting I saw preening its iridescent body in a mud puddle in Swinney Switch to a herd of Brahman bulls that had gathered at dusk near the gate of a fence outside Floresville. In that light the bulls' hides were the color of marble; their pendulous scrotums swayed about the rich grass, and their curious humps twitched when they shifted their weight from one hoof to another. At the gate stood a man in a red cap. He was not doing anything, just standing there with the bulls, and they in turn seemed thoughtlessly drawn to him.

It began to grow dark, in a peaceful, sodden way, as if the air were absorbing darkness rather than relinquishing light. The radio said that the widow of Pancho Villa had died, but then the station disappeared in a flurry of static before I could hear details. I tuned in an ad for Diamond Head water troughs, followed by a self-conscious country song in which Hank Williams, Jr., managed to drop the names of Willie and Waylon and Kris in lamenting the sad fact that nobody wanted to go out and get drunk with him anymore. The night deepened and the voices on the radio grew more desperate:

> You got to look that devil in the eye if you're sufferin' from satanic oppression. You got to say, "Devil, in the name of Jesus of Nazareth, take your hands offa my *finances!*"
>
> And Bob?
>
> Yessir.
>
> I just wanted to say something about this El Salvadorian business.
>
> Sorry. We're about out of time.
>
> I don't see why we just can't take one of them tactical nuclear bombs…
>
> Gotta go.
>
> Now, wait a minute. Put that bomb in downtown Nicaragua or wherever…
>
> Bye…

I coasted home to Austin on the strains of a song about a honky-tonk cowboy who was doomed to a life of loneliness because he couldn't dance the cotton-eyed Joe. I went to bed feeling glum and perplexed, having expected that by now all those images and impressions of Texas would have formed themselves into a single testament. But I was still at arm's length, still mildly estranged. I just couldn't dance the cotton-eyed Joe.

In the morning my five-year-old daughter was whiny and irritable when I took her to school, and after pacing around the house for a while in more or less the same mood I drove back to the school to pick her up.

"Where are we going?" she asked. "To the dentist?"

"No. To Enchanted Rock."

"What's that?"

"It's a special place."

"Oh. Like Disneyland."

We listened to her Little Thinker tape as we drove west through the LBJ country, where the roadside peach vendors were just putting up their stalls, and on through Fredericksburg, with its Sunday houses and German bakeries and relentless old-country quaintness.

The first we saw of Enchanted Rock was a bare salmon-covered nubbin erupting from the serene Hill Country vista ahead. The nubbin quickly loomed larger, until it was clearly a great stone mountain, so huge and abruptly *there* that all perspective dropped away and the rock had the one-dimensional clarity of a scene that has been painted on a panel of glass.

I felt an impatience to be there, to climb to the top. Enchanted Rock was perhaps my favorite Texas place, an immense granite batholith that the Indians had considered sacred. I had found it to be sacred too, and it was to Enchanted Rock that I used to come when I was in an especially powerful sulking mood.

We came quickly to the base of the rock, and about us, as we got out of the car, we could see the deep crease across its brow along which several minute figures crept upward.

"Wow," said my daughter. "Are we going to climb that?"

We were. We jumped across the half-dozen or so separate threads of water that composed Big Sandy Creek and followed the trail upward until it was lost in the expanse of solid rock. Then we walked up at a sharp angle, stopping about every fifteen yards so my daughter could rest and express disbelief at how far we had come. Near the top, where it was very steep, she got a little testy, so I picked her up and carried her to the summit.

"Boy," she said, as I staggered along with her in my arms, "mountain climbing is hard, isn't it?"

Finally I set her down next to a plaque that had been riveted into the rock.

"What does it say?"

"It says, 'Enchanted Rock. From its summit in the fall of 1841, Captain John C. Hays, while surrounded by Comanche Indians who cut him off from his ranging company, repulsed the whole band and inflicted upon them such heavy losses that they fled.'"

"What does that mean?"

"It means a guy had a fight with Indians up here."

"But Indians are nice now, aren't they? They only use their bows and arrows for practice."

Yes, Indians were nice now. Texas itself was nice, no longer a hostile country battled over by contentious spirits, but a reasonably representative American place, filled with familiar and ephemeral things: Wal-Marts, civic ballets, wind surfing, cable TV, Hare Krishnas in business suits. But Texas had not been wholly digested somehow, and in places like Enchanted Rock you could still get a buzz, you could still feel its insistent identity.

From the top the rock was as barren as the moon, and its vast surface canted forward slightly, so that there were two horizons, the rim of the mountain and, beyond it, the edge of the true world. I hoped this sight would take with my daughter; when her sisters were older I would bring them up here too so that Enchanted Rock could seep into their memories. I felt this place belonged to them, more than to me; they were native Texans, after all.

The lag, the missed beat I felt in my relationship with Texas, was something that I trusted would be corrected in future generations. And for the present, Enchanted Rock was every bit as much a power center for me as that sandstone boulder back in Oklahoma City. And there were others: a certain stretch of the Frio River, where after weeks of senseless brooding I had made up my mind to go ahead and be happy and get married; the lobby of the Menger hotel in San Antonio, where there was a plaque dedicated to the memory of Sidney Lanier and where you could find a gigantic Titianesque Nativity scene hung near a painting titled *Venting Cattle on the Frisco Range*; the Indian pictographs in Seminole Canyon; the mud flats and back bays of Laguna Madre; the old Shanghai Jimmy's Chili Rice on Lemmon Avenue in Dallas, where you were served chili by the man who claimed he had introduced that dish to China during the Boxer Rebellion; the Chinati Mountains; the Flower Gardens coral reef; the thick, suffocating Big Thicket forests, where you could find quicksand and wild orchids; any number of places that would give you all the barbeque you could eat for $7 or $8, where you could sit beneath a pressed-tin ceiling on a humid midsummer evening, give the baby a rib bone to gnaw on to help her with her teething, and pursue the illusion that life outside Texas would be bland and charmless. Texas for me was a thousand things like that, a thousand moments that in my mind had been charged with a special quality of place that I could not explain or understand. I only knew that the quality, and the place, was Texas.

A fault line ran across the back of Enchanted Rock like the stitching on a baseball. There was a sort of cave there, illuminated by the gaps between the collapsed boulders that had formed it, where we went to drink our apple juice. My daughter announced she wanted to play Indian.

"You be the daddy Indian," she said. "You can be taking a nap while I make tea."

I closed my eyes obediently and felt the cool air of the cave on my face. I let the whole Texas question rest. "I'll just make some people who like it this way," God had said. I wasn't sure if I had been put on the earth with an inborn love for Texas, but I certainly seemed to have a high tolerance for it. Lying there in the cave, on the summit of an ancient and hallowed mountain, I still felt a mild longing to live someplace that was more exotic, or more ordinary; someplace that was not Texas. One of these days I might do that. Just not today.

INDEX